# New Pioneers
# in the Heartland

# THE NEW IMMIGRANTS SERIES

## Allyn & Bacon

Series Editor, Nancy Foner, State University of New York at Purchase

# New Pioneers In The Heartland:

# Hmong Life In Wisconsin

*Jo Ann Koltyk*
*University of Wisconsin-Rock County*

Allyn and Bacon
Boston • London • Toronto • Sydney • Tokyo • Singapore

Series Editor: Sarah L. Dunbar
Editor-in-Chief, Social Science: Karen Hanson
Series Editorial Assistant: Elissa V. Schaen
Marketing Manager: Karon Bowers
Consulting Editor: Sylvia Shepard
Manufacturing Buyer: Suzanne Lareau
Cover Designer: Jenny Hart
Editorial-Production Service: Omegatype Typography, Inc.

ISBN: 0-205-27412-9

Printed in the United States of America.
10 9 8 7 6          02

**Photo Credits:** Jo Ann Koltyk

**Cover Photo:** Hmong women and a day of picture-taking in
the park.

# Contents

# Photographs

# Foreword to the Series

The United States is now experiencing the largest wave of immigration in the country's history. The 1990s, it is predicted, will see more new immigrants enter the United States than in any decade in American history. New immigrants from Asia, Latin America, and the Caribbean are changing the American ethnic landscape.

Until recently, immigration was associated in the minds of many Americans with the massive influx of southern and eastern Europeans at the turn of the century. Since the late 1960s, America has again become a country of large-scale immigration, this time attracting newcomers from developing societies of the world. The number of foreign-born is at an all-time high: nearly twenty million foreign-born persons were counted in the 1990 census. Although immigrants are a smaller share of the nation's population than they were earlier in the century—8 percent in 1990 compared to about 15 percent in 1910–recent immigrants are having an especially dramatic impact because their geographic concentration is greater today. About half of all immigrants entering the United States during the 1980s moved to eight urban areas: Los Angeles, New York, Miami, Anaheim, Chicago, Washington, D.C., Houston, and San Francisco. America's major urban centers are, increasingly, immigrant cities with new ethnic mixes.

Who are the new immigrants? What are their lives like here? How are they redefining themselves and their cultures? And how are they contributing to a new and changing America? The *New Immigrants Series* provides a set of case studies that explores these themes among a variety of groups. Each book in the series is written by a recognized expert who has done extensive in-depth ethnographic research on one of the immigrant groups. The groups represent a broad range of today's arrivals, coming from a variety of countries and cultures. The studies cover a wide geographical range as well, based on research done in different parts of the country, from New York to California.

Most of the books in the series are written by anthropologists. All draw on qualitative research that shows what it means to be an immigrant in America today. As part of each study, individual immigrants tell their stories, which will help give a sense of the experience and problems of the newcomers. Through the case studies, a dynamic picture emerges of the way immigrants are carving out new lives for themselves at the same time as they are creating a new and more diverse America.

The ethnographic case study, long the anthropologist's trademark, provides a depth often lacking in research on immigrants in the United States. Many anthropologists, moreover, like a number of authors in the *New Immigrants Series,* have done research in the sending society as well as in the United States. Having field experience at both ends of the migration chain makes anthropologists particularly sensitive to the role of transnational ties that link immigrants to their home societies. With first-hand experience of immigrants in their home culture, anthropologists are also well positioned to appreciate continuities as well as changes in the immigrant setting.

As the United States faces a growing backlash against immigration, and many Americans express ambivalence and sometimes hostility toward the latest arrivals, it becomes more important than ever to learn about the new immigrants and to hear their voices. The case studies in the *New Immigrants Series* will help readers understand the cultures and lives of the newest Americans and bring out the complex ways the newcomers are coming to terms with and creatively adapting to life in a new land.

NANCY FONER
Series Editor

# Preface

This study examines one of our newest immigrant groups in the United States, the Hmong refugees from Laos. In ethnographic fashion, the reader is presented with an intimate portrait of Hmong family life in Wisconsin. The book first traces the stages of the Hmong refugee experience and then looks at how Hmong families are adjusting and adapting to their new lives in the United States. The primary focus is on daily life routines. From this perspective one gains an appreciation of Hmong kinship networks and community. Women's activities are woven throughout this study to highlight the roles they play in their family's social and economic adaptation. From a family centered focus, the reader gains an appreciation for how the Hmong see their own adaptational process and how they represent and define their Hmongness in the United States.

# Acknowledgments

I wish to thank all the Hmong people who helped to make this book possible. Their kindness, generosity, and sincere interest in seeing my research come to fruition is deeply appreciated. By allowing me into their life they have given me the gift of understanding my own family and American culture and society in a new way. It is a gift of wisdom which I will never be able to repay. Special thanks as well to the Wausau Hmong Mutual Association and the Hmong Christian and Missionary Alliance Church for their warm and cooperative assistance and for making me feel at home in Wausau.

This research was made possible with the support of a pre-doctoral grant (#5362) from the Wenner Gren Foundation for Anthropological Research. A major portion of Chapter seven was previously published and is reprinted by permission of the American Folklore Society from the *Journal of American Folklore 106* (422), Fall 1993, and may not be reproduced.

I owe a special thanks to my graduate school advisors at the University of Wisconsin, Madison—Jack Kugelmass, Herbert S. Lewis, and Lois A. Anderson—for their encouragement and criticism of my ideas. Many thanks as well to the faculty, staff, and students at the University of Wisconsin-Rock County campus in Janesville, Wisconsin for providing such a pleasant atmosphere in which to teach and write. Janet LaBrie, Mary Schlais, Maryann Maloney, Karen Atwood, and Julia Hornbostel have been especially helpful. My sincerest thanks goes to the editors, Nancy Foner and

Sylvia Shepard, whose keen editorial skills and suggestions have helped immensely in transforming several drafts into this polished version for publication.

Finally I thank my husband, John T. Miller for his emotional support and encouragement throughout this long, and at times, arduous journey.

This book is in memory of my paternal grandparents who immigrated to America from Poland in 1907.

# Refugee Resettlement and the Hmong

**M**arathon County Park, near the heart of the city of Wausau, Wisconsin seems at first glance to represent a slice of traditional American middle-class life in the heartland. The heavily forested park contains walking trails, camping and picnic areas, baseball fields, an indoor ice arena, and a children's wading pool. In the evenings, the park comes alive with all the sounds and smells of community life, from Little League games and family picnics, to weekly band concerts, 4-H fairs, and summer carnivals. The smell of hot dogs and fries from the year-round concession booth drifts up through the night air. People linger around tables, eating hamburgers and ice cream cones. Others line up to buy tickets to ride on the miniature train or the merry-go-round, which belts out Polka music.

If one looks a little further, however, it becomes clear that Marathon County Park is also a favorite gathering place for Wausau's newest arrivals: Hmong refugees from Laos. On my first evening in Wausau in June of 1991, I was advised to visit Marathon County park as a way of meeting Hmong people. The parks, I was told by a native of the city, were being "taken over by the Hmong." However, no Hmong were visible in the park until I walked towards the back. There I found a large crowd of over one hundred Hmong gathered in what appeared to be some sort of celebration. As I learned later, this was just a normal, informal gathering at the park—part of everyday life for Hmong in Wausau.

Cars and vans jammed the parking area. Hmong children were everywhere, playing on the monkey bars, on the squeaky swings and teeter totters, on the ground and grass. Some had brought their bicycles and tricycles. Small boys roamed together, arms around each other, squatting here and there to play a game of marbles. A group of small girls sat on the grass playing a Hmong game of tossing small stones in the air (similar to jacks) and then trying to catch them on the backs of their hands. Further over, a group of men were playing kickball (*kotaw*) and another playing a game of volleyball.

Along the side lines sat wives and other womenfolk, huddled in small groups talking, watching, listening, or nursing babies. Some sat on the tailgates of their cars, some in the backs of their vans, others sat at picnic tables. A group of older men, in their fifties, sat hunched over a picnic table playing cards, while teenagers roamed around the outskirts of the area, heads tucked down and hands in their pockets, talking and whispering in English.

Several women sat near coolers, selling soda from the trunks of their cars. One woman was scooping out a dessert made of multi-colors of tapioca, coconut milk and ice cubes (called *nab vaam*) into plastic bowls. The dessert comes from the Lao but was adopted and transformed by the Hmong while they were in the refugee camps. It has acquired great popularity as one of the foods sold during Hmong fairs, soccer festivals, or other special occasions.

Throughout Wausau, parks have become favorite places for Hmong families, where they have soccer and volleyball matches and tournaments, socialize, walk, and take photographs that they can send to relatives living in other locations.

## WHO ARE THE HMONG?

The first Hmong families began arriving in Wausau in 1976, shortly after the Vietnam War ended. Ever since this time, the city has had the largest concentration of Hmong in Wisconsin. The Hmong are the most recent arrivals in a long line of immigrant groups who have settled in Wausau, beginning with German immigrants well over one hundred years ago. When the Hmong started arriving to Wausau most people had never heard of them. "Who are the Hmong?" and "Why are they here?" were the most frequently asked questions.

The majority of the six million Hmong in the world live in China, their original homeland. Hmong history can be traced as far back as 2700 B.C. when they were first mentioned in Chinese historical records (Savina, 1930). Early Chinese writings refer to the Hmong as the *San Miao* (or Three Miao) and accuse them of being troublemakers because they attacked the expanding Chinese settlements that were encroaching their lands in the basin of the Yellow River in Southwest China (Mottin, 1980: 16).

Historical records continue to reflect the Hmong as a people on the move, being pushed out of areas in China by expanding *Han* dynasties, or resettling in new areas to avoid conflict with the *Han* government over taxation and policies that imposed control over their lifestyle. Revolts and wars over taxation continued throughout the eighteenth and nineteenth century. Finally, a Hmong defeat in the early nineteenth century drove out about one-seventh of the three million Hmong that were in China at that time. The Hmong began moving into Indochina around 1810 to settle in Vietnam and Laos, and then in Thailand (Mottin, 1980: 37).

Rebellions over taxation continued as the Hmong in Laos struggled to maintain their independence from the French colonial government. Rebellions first occurred in 1896 and again in 1918. During World War II the Hmong became divided, with leaders from two main groups, the Ly clan (represented by Touby Ly Foung) and the Lo clan (represented by Lo Fay Dang). The Ly clan sided with the French while the Lo clan joined forces with the Japanese. After the war, the Hmong remained divided.

Civil war in Laos was intermittent from 1949 to 1975. The division among the Hmong was again reflected by the Ly clan siding with the French, the Royal Lao Government, and then finally allying with the Americans during the Vietnam War, under the Hmong leadership of General Vang Pao. The Lo clan supported the Pathet Lao (communist forces) and the North Vietnamese.

In the 1960s the Hmong were recruited by the United States Army as a special force of guerilla fighters to control the mountainous border regions between Laos and North Vietnam and to block the movement of communist forces and supplies. Funds from the Central Intelligence Agency supplied arms, ammunition, and food to the Hmong for their alliance and support.

By the end of April 1975, with the collapse of Saigon and the pullout of U.S. troops, the United States abruptly terminated their support to General Vang Pao and the secret army. Unable to defend their territory without United States support, the Hmong became direct targets of persecution by the newly established Lao People's Democratic Republic. Physical and genocidal attacks against the Hmong caused many connected to U.S. military operations to flee into Thailand for their safety. Further refugee flows resulted when the Lao People's Democratic Republic instituted re-education camps, land reform policies and forced settlement. Farm and work co-operatives were established in which the majority of the Hmong's rice crop was taken to support government taxes and village rice banks. The economic consequences of not having sufficient amounts of food to feed their families created yet a second wave of refugees out of Laos.[1]

Many of the Hmong from Laos have resettled in the West after spending varying lengths of time in refugee camps in Thailand, in which the main camp for the Hmong was Ban Vinai. The Hmong reside primarily in the United States and Canada. Some have also been resettled in Australia, France, and French Guyana. The 1990 U.S. census counted over 100,000 Hmong in the United States.

## THE IMPACT OF THE HMONG IN WAUSAU

Wausau lies in the heart of Wisconsin about two hours north of Madison. The Wisconsin River threads its course along Route 51 like a ribbon and then cuts its way into the center of the city. Rib Mountain, one of the highest points in Wisconsin, stands just outside the city and serves as a tourist attraction for skiing during the winter months and camping and hiking during the summer. Nestled within a landscape of hills, valleys, wooded areas, and farmland, Wausau appears to be a quiet, safe, comfortable, and tranquil community with plenty of open spaces for recreation or solitude. Out of human compassion to help victims of war, the Wausau community began sponsoring Hmong families in 1976. Initially sponsorship was through various church groups, especially Lutheran and Catholic social services.

When I arrived to do my pilot study in 1988 there were about 1500 Hmong people living in the Wausau area. A few years later when I was conducting my dissertation research, from June 1991 to May 1992, the Hmong population in the Wausau area had reached 3128 people, a figure representing almost 10 percent of the city's estimated 32,000 residents. As of 1996, the population had grown to 4200 or about 11 percent of the city total.

The effect of Hmong migration to Wausau has been felt in practically every aspect of the community, from law enforcement and legal issues, to housing, education and development, social and welfare programs, economic and political structures, and in the medical community. At every level, the community has been faced with an immigrant group whose belief systems, in many ways, differ radically from their own. Doctors have been challenged by cultural differences in the interpretation of illness and treatment. Legal institutions have been confronted by such diverse cultural traditions as early teen marriages, bride capture, polygyny, disciplining of children, herbal practices, and religious beliefs in shamanism and animal sacrifice.

Neighbors are confused as well about the Hmong, especially from what they can see of the daily lifestyles of their newest neighbors. The Hmong's large extended families and high birth rates along with their use of welfare programs have incited a host of emotional feelings, ranging from concern to prejudice, anger, bitterness, and hostility.

In 1980 Wausau was an ethnically homogeneous city with less than one percent of the population as non-white (Beck, 1994a: 86). Then, Wausau residents described their city as cozy, safe, and middle-class, easily fitting the image of the American dream. Today, many of these residents look on in disbelief in what they see as an "invasion" of their neighborhoods and city. One non-Hmong resident who rents apartments to Hmong families told me that he would not mind the Hmong being in Wausau if they were not so visible, "But my gosh", he exclaimed "They are now on every corner and block that you can see. They're in our malls and at Shopko, and just all over."

Not only do many of the residents describe their new Hmong neighbors as "strange", but also some would like to see their city the way it was before the Hmong arrived. Others are embittered by the benefits that the Hmong get as refugees. With limited jobs in the area, over 60 percent of the Hmong at the time of my research were still receiving public assistance and English language and job training. Non-Hmong residents hold up images of their own immigrant ancestors who had to work hard; there were no handouts back then, they say.

## THE WAUSAU COMMUNITY

The word Wausau comes from a native American Indian word meaning "far-away." But the more popularized version of the word comes from television commercials in which Wausau Insurance Company, the community's largest employer, advertises the

proper spelling and pronounciation of their city: It's Wausau not
Warsaw…and that's spelled W-A-USA-U, with U.S.A. in the mid-
dle." The name is symbolically significant in a number of ways.
Wausau is indeed far away in terms of the Hmong homeland of
Laos. But it also represents the heartland of America, having been
named the best all-American city in the U.S.A. in 1984.

I chose Wausau as a research site for several reasons. The population in the Wausau area is basically white, from German and
other European backgrounds with few minorities present until the
arrival of the Hmong. Cambodians, Lowland Lao, and Vietnamese
refugees also reside in Wausau, but their numbers are small; they
are only about 7 percent of the total Southeast Asian refugee population in the area. The Hmong are now the predominant ethnic
and minority group in Wausau. Wausau offers an ideal setting for
examining the dynamics of race, ethnicity, culture, and immigration in the United States.

Wausau's size and location was also attractive. I wanted to examine Hmong adaptation in a small-city setting. Most immigrant
studies have been conducted in large cities like New York, Los Angeles, and Miami, where problems of adaptation are compounded
by problems of living in a metropolitan area. Few studies have
been done on the Hmong living in small cities in rural areas of the
United States and hardly anything has been written on the Hmong
in rural Wisconsin (see Mitchell, et al., 1989; Hutchison, 1992).

The Hmong population in Wausau consisted of thirteen different clans with a demographic mix of families in terms of age, gender, and varying lengths of arrival and residency in the United
States.[2] The percentage of Christian and non-Christian Hmong
was about 50–50, and the two major dialect groups—the White
Hmong (*Hmoob Dawb*) and Blue/Green Hmong (*Moob Ntsuab*)—
were present.[3]

The Wausau area consists of a collection of municipalities including the town of Rib Mountain, Stettin, the City of Schofield,
the Village of Rothschild, and the Town of Weston and Kronewet-
ter. Altogether, the area has a population of about 70,000 people.
The greatest concentration of Hmong residents is found within the
city of Wausau itself and scattered in ethnic pockets on all sides.

Manufacturing, especially of paper, lumber and building
products, is the cornerstone of the Wausau economy, but agricul-
ture is also important in the area. Marathon County is one of the
leading producers of dairy products in the United States, known

especially for its cheese products. Ginseng is another leading product in Marathon County. The county provides about 95 percent of the nation's cultivated ginseng, which is exported to Asian countries for medicinal use.

The Wausau community is the regional center for the North Central part of Wisconsin, serving the area with three television stations, a daily newspaper, eight radio stations, and a regional medical and airport facility. The city is also home to the University of Wisconsin-Marathon campus, one of twenty-six campuses in the UWc System. The North Central Technical Institute is also in Wausau and serves residents from throughout Marathon County.

Wausau's central location within the state makes for easy travel to all the other major cities in Wisconsin. The cities of Appleton, Eau Claire, Green Bay, LaCrosse, Madison, and Milwaukee are only several hours away and all have sizable Hmong populations. Larger cities like Chicago and the twin cities of St. Paul and Minneapolis are within a four hour drive. Hmong families in Wausau frequently travel back and forth to these cities to visit with their relatives. Likewise, Hmong families all over the midwest and elsewhere travel to Wausau to maintain their kinship obligations.

If Wausau's location enables the Hmong to remain in touch with relatives in nearby cities, it also is a safe community, one with low crime, affordable housing, and good schools. A Hmong woman who has lived in Wausau for over eight years told me that she liked having access to the stores and yet being able to get away from the hurried life by driving just a few minutes out of town to her garden in the country. The peacefulness of having the river, mountain, and open space appealed to her and her husband, and reminded her of her homeland.

Part of Wausau's peacefulness stems from the many parks and recreational areas throughout the city and in Marathon county. Residents and tourists alike take advantage of these nature areas which often offer a wide variety of summer and winter activities including fishing, camping, hiking, boating, swimming, picnicking, baseball, skiing, and ice skating. Hmong families utilize these parks as communal backyards. They are places where they can meet in groups to socialize on a daily basis.

Wausau has its share of clubs and voluntary associations. Almost every Christian denomination has a church in Wausau; Lutheran and Catholic churches predominate. There is also a Jewish synagogue, and now a Hmong Christian and Missionary Alliance church, built in 1990, with a membership of well over 500.

Real estate in the area is still affordably priced. In 1992 one could still find a two and three bedroom home in the $40–50,000 range, including duplexes which were popular among the Hmong buying their first homes.

Many state and federal programs are also located in Wausau and assist the Hmong in the resettlement process. Human service agencies include English as a Second Language programs, Hmong Refugee Resettlement Community Development, Refugee Health, Refugee Services, and the Wausau Area Hmong Mutual Association.

With four Hmong food stores, a quarterly Hmong newsletter, a weekly radio broadcast in the Hmong language, Hmong language and culture classes, Hmong-initiated informational groups, and an active Hmong social life within the community, many Hmong feel very connected to their new Wausau home. Just as Wausau is being dramatically transformed by the influx of Hmong to the area, the Hmong are also being reshaped by their experiences in Wausau. This ethnography examines family and social life among the Hmong as they make new lives in the heartland of the United States.

## THE HMONG IN CONTEXT OF THE INDOCHINESE REFUGEES DIASPORA

Over one and a half million Indochinese refugees from Vietnam, Laos, and Kampuchea (formerly Cambodia) have arrived on U.S. shores since the fall of Saigon in 1975. The Indochinese refugees include six major ethnic groups: Vietnamese, ethnic Chinese from Vietnam, Khmer from Kampuchea, and ethnic Lao, Mien, and Hmong from Laos.

The Refugee Act of 1980 classifies an individual as a refugee when he or she is unable to remain or return to his or her country of origin because of "persecution or well-founded fear of persecution on account of race, religion, nationality, membership in a particular social group, or political opinion" (Haines, 1985: 10). Immigrants are distinguished from refugees by the fact that immigrants have voluntarily chosen to emigrate.

The pre-migration experiences of refugees often differ from those of immigrants, especially in terms of the nature of their departure from their home country and the time spent in refugee camps before resettlement takes place. In the case of the Hmong, escape from Laos was dangerous and traumatic for most. Long stays in refugee camps marked by cramped and crowded conditions and deprivation of food and basic necessities also define Hmong pre-migration experiences.

Refugees are eligible for special government-funded programs to aid their adjustment, whereas immigrants are not. Despite this, Nazli Kibria suggests that we "consider refugees as a type of immigrant" because "there is considerable overlap in experience between the two groups" once they arrive at their final destination (1993: 12).

The major policy concerns about Indochinese refugees have been their initial resettlement and adjustment to the United States, and their capacity to achieve economic self-sufficiency (Strand and Jones, 1985). In resettling Indochinese refugees, the U.S. government made two decisions: to provide cash and social benefits to the refugees, and to disperse them around the country so as not to create a financial burden upon any one state. The Indochina Migration and Refugee Assistance Act of 1975 authorized federal funds for two years to assist in the Indochinese resettlement. The Act provided cash, medical, educational, and social service assistance in the form of federal reimbursements to local and state agencies (Taft, et al., 1979).

The decision to disperse Indochinese refugees around the country was based on the U.S. government's previous experiences with Cuban refugees. Cuban refugees had remained clustered in Miami in the early 1960s, despite attempts to resettle them in areas outside the Miami area (Taft, et al., 1979; Haines, 1982: 174). It was believed that dispersing Indochinese refugees would minimize any negative economic impact that they might have on local communities and on county and state budgets. The dispersal strategy also held the promise that many small ethnic communities would form in different locations as subsequent refugees came to America under the family reunification program (Fass, 1991).

But the dispersal strategy backfired, exemplifying the importance of family, kinship, and ethnic ties in the adjustment and support of newly arriving refugees. Almost immediately after

Indochinese refugees were dispersed, they began a series of internal or "secondary" migrations within the United States, seeking out relatives and friends of their own ethnic backgrounds and clustering in key areas to form ethnic communities. The secondary migrations were to states in the west and south, and towards areas with relatively large refugee populations (Haines, 1982: 175). Various explanations for these secondary migrations have been suggested: the pull of employment opportunities and established ethnic communities; more generous welfare benefits, better training opportunities, the congenial climates of some states; as well as the desire to reunite with relatives (U.S. Dept. of Health and Human Services, 1992: 50).

In 1979 over 70 per cent of all Indochinese refugees lived in twelve states. California had the greatest share (32.6%), followed by Texas (8.7%), Washington (4.4%), Illinois (3.7%), Minnesota (3.4%), New York (2.9%), and smaller percentages in Florida, Massachusetts, and Wisconsin (Fass, 1991: 4). This spatial distribution remained basically the same in the early 1990s. California ranked number one as a resettlement site for refugees from all three Indochinese countries for 1991. Approximately 396,000 Indochinese refugees (or about 40%) live in California.

Outside of California, each group of Indochinese refugees was drawn to particular states through secondary migration. The second most popular location for Cambodians in the 1980s was Pennsylvania; for Vietnamese, Texas; and for refugees from Laos, Minnesota. Wisconsin ranked third for Laotian refugees, the majority of whom were Hmong (U.S. Department of Health and Human Services, 1992: 7). More recent population figures show that Wisconsin now ranks second and Minnesota third for the Hmong population (Fass, 1991). The Hmong population in Wisconsin, as of June 1994, was estimated at about 31,327.

Although they are often lumped together by policy analysts, Indochinese refugees are not a homogeneous group. Each of the six ethnic groups has its own particular cultural traditions and belief systems. Furthermore, the groups vary in their level of exposure to Western culture and in the degree of preparation for entering U.S. society. Variations also exist among and within the groups in terms of the particular time that they fled from their country, the amount of time spent in refugee camps, and the social and economic climate in the United States when they arrived.

Many first-wave male Indochinese refugees, who came between 1975 and 1978, were connected to U.S. military operations as soldiers, advisors, and officials. After short stays in refugee camps, they were resettled in the United States. Although they sometimes needed retraining, most were able to find employment in this country. Many had to take jobs that were lower in status than those they held in their home country, but most were able to become economically self-sufficient quickly.

The occupational profile of Indochinese refugees changed dramatically, however, with the second wave of refugees beginning in the fall of 1978 and continuing to the present. While the first wave refugees were mainly Vietnamese and from urban areas, the second wave were predominantly from rural backgrounds—peasant farmers, fisherman, and hilltribe people, including the Hmong. Refugees in the second wave were much younger as a group, had larger families, and lacked the educational and occupational skills necessary for a post-industrial U.S. job market (Strand and Jones, 1985: 35).

Many of the second-wave refugees, like the Hmong, either came from an oral-based culture with no familiarity in literacy, or they were marginally literate with little or no familiarity with written forms of communication. Their pre-migration experiences included severe trauma from war and escape and lengthy stays in refugee camps where dependency, idleness, impermanence, and an orientation towards the past rather than the future were the rule (Stein 1981).

Also, the social climate for the second wave refugees and their families was not so favorable as it was for the first wave. With many out of work during the 1980's recession, accusations were made that the Indochinese were taking away jobs and other valuable benefits that first belonged to U.S. citizens.

Second-wave refugees do have one advantage compared to their predecessors who arrived before 1978. Refugees in the first wave had no pre-existing settlement group in America to guide them when they arrived. Government-funded programs for training and assistance, sponsors, voluntary agencies, and government-assisted mutual aid associations took the role that would have otherwise fallen to pre-existing groups. These agencies did not always understand the complexity of a group's cultural heritage and value system, or how their family and kinship systems helped refugees adjust during the resettlement process.

## FIELDWORK AMONG THE HMONG

My initial research with the Hmong began as a pilot health project in Wausau in 1988. From this experience I decided to do my dissertation research on the Hmong in Wisconsin. From 1988 to 1991 I worked closely with a Hmong woman, Mrs. Chia A., and her family in Madison.[4] Chia gave me Hmong language lessons, invited me to participate in a wide variety of family and kin activities, and became one of my main informants in Madison. Chia and her family's membership in the Hmong Christian and Missionary Alliance Church broadened my understanding of their beliefs and the tensions that exist between Christian and non-Christian Hmong in America.[5]

My connection to Chia and her family was invaluable to me personally and in my understanding of Hmong culture when I returned to Wausau in 1991 to do this study. In fact, Chia and her husband introduced me and my research plans to the Hmong Christian and Missionary Alliance Church in Wausau. The pastor of the church asked the members to assist me in my study in any way that they could. As a result, I was able to meet people involved in the Hmong Mutual Association in Wausau, which, in turn, asked the Hmong community to welcome me. Finally, by giving me the Hmong name *Kaab Npauj* (pronounced Kang Bao) Chia tied me to her family while at the same time, bestowed upon me a symbolic calling card that communicated to the Hmong in Wausau my attributes and character as a person and my sincerity to learn about Hmong ways.[6]

I was fortunate to find an apartment in one of the areas where Hmong cluster. Hmong families lived all around me within a ten block radius. I became acquainted with them as neighbor, friend, researcher, and as a volunteer ESL (English as Second Language) teacher at the local neighborhood drop-in center, called the Neighbor's Place. Living within the neighborhood and frequenting the local stores, gave me access to daily routines and an introduction to a wide circle of Hmong. I was a frequent visitor to Sunday Church services both at the Hmong Christian and Missionary Alliance Church and at the Catholic Hmong services, which were held in the afternoons for Hmong worshipers. Grocery stores, laundromats, public parks, shopping centers, hospitals, clinics, car repair shops and other local facilities all provided natural settings in which to observe the behavior of the residents of the area.

It did not take me long to find out that the city was clearly divided between Hmong and non-Hmong participation during many public events. There were two worlds existing in a single location, with very little overlap of Hmong and non-Hmong, except for the sharing of school grounds and public facilities. Even then, social boundaries were exhibited in places such as the public parks, the mall, churches, and homes.

Informal visiting with my Hmong neighbors afforded me the opportunity to observe family patterns, daily activities, consumption and spending behavior, and attitudes about life in the United States. As my neighbors came to trust me, I was invited to attend ceremonies, celebrations, rituals, and other family gatherings. Through formal and informal interviews I was able to obtain life history narratives as well as information from shamans, herbalists, masseuses, magic specialists, musicians, and needlework specialists.

My volunteer job as an ESL teacher at the Neighbor's Place was also beneficial to my study. The center had initiated a program to teach the Hmong women English and basic cultural information about the United States. Over twenty Hmong women from all clans, age groups, religious beliefs, and with varying lengths of residency in the United States participated at this center. Although I only taught one afternoon per week, I sat in on other teachers' classes to assist and observe. Word spread throughout the Hmong community that I was the ESL teacher who could speak Hmong and who understood Hmong culture. The role allowed for a much greater exposure in the community and opened up opportunities for visiting with women and families not connected to the drop-in center.

## Problems in Fieldwork: Impression Management

One of the main problems an anthropologist faces is gaining the trust of those she is observing. The process of building trust and obtaining information was especially complicated among the Hmong in Wausau.

The Hmong are acutely concerned about the impression they give outsiders. Since the Hmong arrived in America, the media has sensationalized them as a "primitive" and "backward hill-tribe" people. Hmong oral based traditions, their lack of written forms of communication until the early 1950s, and their practices of shamanism and ancestor worship are just some of the traditions the media highlight to explain Hmong problems and adjustment to U.S. life. Sudden death syndrome, which causes healthy Hmong men to die in their sleep, along with high fertility rates, early marriages, and bride capture, all add to an "exotic" view of the Hmong.

As the Hmong have learned that aspects of their culture seem primitive or offensive to many Americans, they have become reluctant to talk to outsiders about them. For instance, the Hmong community is secretive and evasive about such practices as early marriages, polygyny, bride capture, disciplining of children, herbal practices, and shamanism. This does not mean that the Hmong are not concerned about problems that these practices may cause in the United States. They are concerned, but problems usually get discussed in their own circles or at Hmong-organized conferences where outsiders are usually not present or are in the minority.

To manage a "positive" image, one devoid of the kind of sensationalism created by the media, many Hmong resort to strategies of censorship, restricting outsider's access to certain information and cultural practices, while at the same time developing overt displays of traditions that are cast in ways that are acceptable to the dominant group. This is what Lyman and Douglass (1973: 347–48) call "collective impression management," as members of an ethnic group "seek to defuse potentially dangerous aspects of the stereotype in order to arouse sympathy for their position as a minority, and influence outsiders toward a more appreciative and tolerant attitude".

It took several months before people would tell me about shamanism and other customs. One family I knew well told me to talk to their uncle who was a shaman, but when I went to his house he denied knowledge of shamanism. He said he had given up shamanism long ago and become a Christian "just like you Americans." It was only later, when I got to know him well, that he explained that he was afraid that sacrificing an animal was illegal in the United States. He did not want to get in trouble with the law by letting me know he did these things.

Herb use for medicinal purposes was another subject I had to approach with care. Researchers have found high lead counts in the blood of many Hmong babies who were given herbal remedies before coming to the hospital for treatment (see Chun and Deinard 1986). Despite Hmong arguments that their art is centuries old, the U.S. medical profession labeled it, in this case, to be harmful to children. A sense of panic developed about growing and using herbs for remedies; many Hmong were now unsure if these remedies were illegal by U.S. standards. Hence, Hmong fears of discussing herbal use with strangers were understandable. Even when I became familiar with many plants that were being used as medicines, I would be told by families that the plants in their windows were simply flowers to look at "like the Americans have in their homes."

There was also the problem of family members attempting to control and censor life stories especially if they presented a negative image of the group to an outsider. One elderly man was explaining to me how he had learned to play the *kheng* (*qeej*), a musical instrument played at funeral ceremonies to guide spirits of the deceased on their journey home. While recalling this story he suddenly remembered a traumatic experience that he had had as an orphaned child. The man's wife immediately stopped his conversation by saying "Don't tell that to her."

Hmong interpreters also carefully constructed translations, using polite words rather than slang and taking care in how they phrased the subject under discussion. Mention of a second wife, for instance, might be translated as "cousin", "relative", or even "wife's sister" by the interpreter, thus distorting the context of the family and household. Not until I became familiar with the households did I learn the true kinship connections.

I found a direct correlation between length of time in the United States and a reflexive concern to guard the group's self image. Families that were in the United States for three years or less were more open with me and less concerned about impression management. They had not yet learned enough about U.S. culture to feel self-conscious about their own culture.[7] The families here the longest, and who had developed knowledge about mainstream values, attitudes, and practices, were, at first, the hardest to interview and observe. Yet as I gained the trust of more and more families, the issue of censorship began to fade. In fact, many families began to share intimate details of their lives—about which I never would have asked.

As a whole, my richest data were obtained when I went to visit families without an interpreter. My Hmong was passable and functional, but not fluent. I forfeited one kind of information derived from formal interviewing for a more intimate look at the functioning of the family. Participant observation in these settings allowed me a view of family life without placing me at the center as a guest or interviewing "official."

Although my research "officially" ended May 31, 1992 when I moved out of my apartment in Wausau and returned to my home in Janesville, it still continues in many ways. Unlike the researcher who goes to a foreign country for a specified number of months to do fieldwork and then returns home leaving his informants far away, the domestic researcher is still physically connected to his fieldwork site; informants call and invitations to parties and celebrations are still initiated.

After returning to Janesville I became involved with the Janesville Literacy Council, becoming an ESL tutor for a Lao family and meeting other members of the Lao and Cambodian community in Janesville. The insights gained from these contacts and experiences have, I believe, deepened my analysis of the Hmong in Wisconsin.

## WIDER CONNECTIONS BEYOND WISCONSIN

There have been many images and stereotypes about the Hmong in the United States. The most prominent image is the one which predicts their inevitable entrapment in a cycle of poverty and welfare because they lack the educational and occupational skills necessary for economic success in a post-modern world. Some researchers have painted a gloomy picture of Hmong prospects for success in the United States. One historian's remarks about Indochinese refugees is worth quoting:

> Even poorer, as groups, are the Laotians, the Cambodians, and such pre-modern peoples as the Hmong. Few Laotians and Cambodians and no Hmong were really equipped to cope with modern urban society before they left Southeast Asia.... Many of those most directly involved with these refugees fear that they, or most of them, will become a permanent part of that other America where poverty and deprivation are the rule rather than the exception. (Daniels, 1990: 369–370).

Images like these are too simple and they are misleading. They fail to delineate the realities of Hmong daily life in the United States. They do not capture the life experiences of individuals or families and the decisions they make within the context of their new lives in the United States.

This ethnography examines Hmong life from the vantage point of individuals, their families and the communities in which they live. Its primary focus is on daily routines, including work, home life, leisure activities, religious practices, and the attitudes and values that the Hmong hold as newcomers to a new land. I investigate the everyday world through the realm of household decision-making, household economies, kinship networking, and strategies used for economic adaptation. I am especially concerned with the daily lives of Hmong women and women's roles in their family's economic adaptation in the immigration process (see Seller, 1987).

Although this is a study of the Hmong in Wisconsin, the Hmong have important connections and contacts outside of this state—in the country as a whole and beyond. In the literature of traditional anthropology, "community" is often articulated as a literal entity (Cohen, 1985) with a well-defined boundary or territory (Helmreich 1992: 243). However much anthropologists wish to draw a boundary around a group in order to simplify the study of ethnicity, adaptation, and change, the myth of "ethnic closure" is illusive. This study reveals a social world of multiple localities webbed together across national and transnational space (see Appadurai, 1991; Gupta and Ferguson, 1992; Helmreich, 1992).

The Hmong world is flexible and mobile: the Hmong are in constant connection with relatives all over the United States, and the world. Families frequently attend community events in larger cities, and teenagers and unmarried men travel to Hmong communities all around the United States to attend Hmong New Year celebrations or to play in regional volleyball and soccer tournaments. The Hmong church in Wausau sponsors a youth choir on musical tours throughout Wisconsin, Illinois, Kansas City, Michigan, and other Hmong communities. Finally, Hmong return to their homeland for periodic visits, further widening the circle of contact and communication between all Hmong.

Portraying the Hmong in terms of their mobility and within the circle of daily family activities and decision making, provides insight into how the Hmong see their own adaptational process and how they represent and define their Hmongness in the United States. It is from this perspective that this ethnography raises questions about a new group's adjustment and adaptation to the

United States, their acculturation and change, and the role of ethnicity and identity in their lives.

## NOTES

1. For discussions of this time period see Chan, 1994; Adams and McCoy, 1970; Stuart-Fox, 1982; and Quincy, 1988. For further references see the bibliographic works of Olney (1983) and Smith (1988 and 1996).

2. The Hmong follow the patrilineal clan system in which men carry the family's clan name. There are around twenty different clan names in Hmong culture. The clans in Wausau were: Chang, Her, Hang, Kue, Khang, Lee (Ly), Lor (Lo), Moua, Thao, Vang, Vue, Xiong, and Yang.

3. Hmong is a tonal language with eight tones. Both dialects are mutually intelligible and vary only slightly from one another in terms of vocabulary, consonants, vowels, and tone changes. Some words in Blue/Green Hmong contain an additional vowel creating the "ang" and "eng" sounds, and some vowel sounds are eliminated or changed. There are also some vocabulary differences between the two dialects. Scholars may refer to the Blue/Green Hmong as Blue Hmong, Green Hmong, or even Hmong Leng (*Moob Leeg*). Throughout this study I will use the term Blue Hmong.

4. The names used in this ethnography are pseudonyms. I have changed first names and assigned letters to represent the different clan names in order to maintain confidentiality and anonymity of individuals and their lives. Women's clan names have been subsumed under their husband's patrilineal clan, only for ease in reading.

5. The majority of Hmong around the world practice animism and ancestor worship. About half of the Hmong in the U.S., however, practice Christianity.

6. *Kaab Npauj* (or *Kab Npauj* in White Hmong) represents a small bug (*kaab/kab*) in Laos which comes out after the rain and metamorphizes into a beautiful butterfly (*npauj*). Some names have magical or auspicious meanings, or signify the social attributes of a person. The social significance of this name has never been totally revealed to me. However, Hmong reaction to my name has always been one of delight and respect.

7. Many Hmong use the term "American" to describe the racial category of all white non-Hmong people living in America. When they refer to other racial groups they do not usually use the term "American" but instead will say "Blacks", "Mexican", "Chinese", "Indian". Although they realize that these other groups are American citizens, the term "American" takes on the quality of an ethnic/racial group descriptor for the Hmong at this point in time. Many Hmong do not realize that the group they lump together as "American" have ethnic divisions such as Italians, Poles, Jews, etc.

# 2

# The Refugee Experience

**"W**e live in an age of refugees" (Wain, 1981: 9), an age in which world and regional wars and international politics have catapulted millions of people into the status of refugee. Refugees are the "human barometer" of political stability, justice, and order as well as "the core evidence of political failure" (Winter, 1993: 2). The exodus of the Hmong from Laos beginning in 1975 is part of the rapidly growing phenomenon of refugees in the twentieth century.

The term refugee, Roger Zetter notes, "constitutes one of the most powerful labels currently in the repertoire of humanitarian concern, national and international public policy and social differentiation" (1988: 1). It is a term that is associated with some of the most profoundly disturbing human experiences, that of persecution, genocide, dislocation, disruption, forced migration, alienation, and loss.

When the refugee literature is placed alongside the literature on genocides and holocausts, one begins to see that we are also in an "age of atrocity," an age in which bearing witness as victims and survivors radically alters one's life and one's concepts of self (Langer, 1991; Des Pres, 1976; Lifton, 1967). In his autobiography about life in Cambodia under the Pol Pot regime, Haing Ngor writes:

> I have been many things in life. A trader walking barefoot on paths through the jungles. A medical doctor, driving to his clinic in a shiny Mercedes. In the past few years, to the surprise of many people, and above all myself, I have been a Hollywood actor. But nothing has shaped my life as much as surviving the Pol Pot Regime. I am a survivor of the Cambodian holocaust. That's who I am (1987: 1).

Commonly, the voices of those whom war affects the most, the civilian population—the men, women, and children whose lives are dramatically changed by the experience of living in a war-torn country—are left out or silenced by a generalized and often mythologized portrait of war.

Keller (1975), Stein (1981) and others have outlined the major stages of the refugee experience which include the initial perception of a threat, the decision to flee, the period of extreme danger and flight, reaching safety, camp behavior, repatriation, settlement or resettlement, early and late stages of resettlement, adjustment and acculturation, and residual states and changes in behavior caused by the experience (Stein, 1981: 321). Detailed research on each phase can yield information about the unique and generic aspects of the refugee experience. Within these phases we need to know what family life was like, what roles women played within the family and community, how children and elderly individuals were affected, and most importantly, how the experience affected individuals throughout the rest of their lives.

In relating the Hmong refugee experience, I rely on personal narratives told to me during fieldwork in Madison and Wausau. I have organized the narratives into the following three sections: (1) events leading up to and including the individual's escape from Laos (2) refugee camp life and (3) initial resettlement experiences. Some individuals I spoke with expressed feelings of guilt for not having gone through ordeals that most in the group had experienced; others focused their narratives on only one aspect of their experience and remained silent or brief about other aspects. Yet, every individual I talked with was affected in some way by the war, either personally or through links with family members who experienced tragedy.

From these narratives, I hope to give non-Hmong readers an understanding of the individual differences that exist within the Hmong community and how the burden of memory and tragedy is carried into the Hmong resettlement experience and adaptation process.

## EXODUS FROM LAOS

The collective memory of Hmong who escaped from Laos is embedded in the threads of the needlework story cloth (called *paj ntaub*). As history, told through the format of needlework art for a commodity market, the story cloth motifs portray the journey of families crossing mountains, living in jungles, and fleeing enemy soldiers, perilously crossing the Mekong river, and finally reaching the refugee camps. Sally Peterson analyzes the relationship of thematic material in story cloths to collective memory in the following:

> Not all Hmong left Laos by the same route or under the same circumstances, though most recount tales with similar undercurrents of terror. Yet the embroidered, generic version of the escape from Laos has come to represent the collective experience of the Hmong to the outside world, and to many of the Hmong themselves (1988: 11).

More recently, Hmong narratives of escape have been told through the genre of drama, with re-enactments of history, escape, and resettlement told in stage performances[1], and on film in Hmong-produced videos. In both drama and story cloth, the focus is on the collective experience of the group.

The theme of escape in these documents is reinforced by actual personal narratives that Hmong individuals tell of their escape. For instance, Mr. Lee recalled how his family escaped Laos:

> We lived in the jungle for fifteen days with nothing to eat except the leaves we could find. When we went to cross the Mekong River, we were fired on by machine guns. Many people were killed instantly. Arms were blown from shoulders, children died, parents too. Bullets were flying everywhere. We had to travel at night so that the soldiers could not see or hear us, and then we just tried to sleep in the jungle during the day. We finally made it across [the Mekong River] and lived in the camps for four years before coming to America. We've been in America now since 1980.

Other individuals shared similar stories with me, yet each story was different, deeply personal, and in most cases, painful to tell. The narratives drew on memories of past events; they also provided a format for the remembrance of those who did not survive.

An elderly couple in their seventies spoke to me about their experiences in Laos. They had continued to farm after the communists took over Laos. Life was difficult. People had to be cautious, sneaking out to their farmland during the day and hiding in the jungles when the soldiers came to their village. In 1978 soldiers showed up at harvesttime wanting their rice. That is when they decided to leave. There were fifty-two people in their group. They hid in the jungles for three months and then headed toward the border region, preparing to cross the Mekong River. After many unsuccessful attempts and with several family members killed by enemy fire, the family finally crossed the river with makeshift bamboo rafts.

For many Hmong, reflection upon war spans their whole lifetime. Cheng was born in 1952. His life dramatically changed in 1963 when he witnessed his father's brutal death at the hands of enemy soldiers in Laos. In 1978 he fled Laos with his wife and children and then returned to rescue his mother and brother. He recalls: "I went to my mother's village. She and others followed me out. But some were not lucky. My older brother was caught by the Vietnamese and given a poison shot which killed him immediately. And when we were crossing the Mekong again, we were fired on many times."

For some Hmong, escaping Laos was not so difficult or tragic. Many who escaped during the two weeks after the Hmong leader General Vang Pao left in 1975 left the country by a car and boat ride across the river. One man explained:

> My wife and I left Laos for Thailand on June 2nd, 1975. We took a taxi to go to the Mekong River and then we crossed in a boat. This trip cost a lot of money. We had to pay the taxi driver over $100.00 to drive us there.

Many of the refugees who did not have traumatic escapes dwell rather on narratives of arrival and first experiences in the United States.

## REFUGEE CAMP EXPERIENCES

After the dangerous flight from their home country, reaching a refugee camp is the second major phase in the experience of many refugees. Refugees are initiated into a world of camp life which has been described by E. F. Kunz as a "spiritual, spatial, temporal, and emotional equidistant no man's land of midway-to-nowhere" (1973: 133). Refugee camps, one anthropologist writes, "mark physically and symbolically the transition of human beings between societies"(Mortland, 1987: 375). In the case of the Hmong, according to Conquergood, "Their world has been shattered. They are in passage, no longer Laotian, certainly not Thai, and not quite sure where they will end up or what their lives will become" (1988: 180).

Liminal or "betwixt and between" states are appropriate for describing life in refugee camps. As Mortland notes: "The loss and confusion experienced by refugees after separation from their homeland, the unfamiliarity and strangeness of the refugee camps and the uncertainty of the future create an aura of enigma, anxiety and timelessness for the refugee which cannot be overcome as long as they remain in the camps" (1987: 379). A Hmong woman who spent five years of her life in the Ban Vinai refugee camp in Thailand put it this way: "When you are in camp this long you think there is nothing to look forward to, no future. You don't know what will happen to you."

Information about life in the camps was mentioned only in the briefest terms to me. The Hmong themselves are reluctant witnesses.[2] The camp experience was described as being crowded, noisy, and lacking enough food. It is a time period which most say they wish to forget.

Confinement in a refugee camp means a loss of status, identity, and autonomy (Stein, 1981: 324). Only the barest essentials for survival are supplied and the daily routines and relationships once enjoyed cannot be maintained. Not surprisingly, feelings of anxiety, fear, frustration, and emotional disturbance as well as apathy, depression, and aggression are common (Stein, 1981). Conquergood speaks of camp life for the Hmong as representing the opposite of being Hmong—it reduced them from proud, independent, mountain people to landless refugees (1988: 195). Kia, a Hmong woman in her fifties, was one of the few women I met who was willing to describe her camp experience in any detail:

> In Thailand, we were in the camps with wire all around it. There was not enough to eat. We always had to wait in line for food. I remember bags of Koolaid that people were able to buy. But we were too poor to afford it.
>
> Around 8 o'clock every morning, the Thai people let the vendors into the camp to sell things to the Hmong. We would make the *paj ntaub* [needlework] to sell for money, and the relatives would also send us money. That is how we could buy things from the vendors.

> Our house in the camp was very small, one room where 8–12 people shared the space. We cooked outside. And the bathroom was very far away. The water was also very far away. The Thai pump water into the well and let one person have one bucket a day. Three buckets to a family to wash. There were no gardens or anything.My husband worked as a garbage man for the camp. If he worked for one month, they would pay him with toothpaste and soap. Only the school and hospital workers got paid with money. My son worked at the U.N. to help people file paperwork to come to America. Life was very bad in the camp. We were there for nine years.

Conquergood describes Ban Vinai, the principal camp in Thailand for Hmong refugees, as "the largest gathering of Hmong in the world." A population of over 45,000 people, along with animals, spread over 400 acres of undeveloped land:

> Every family seemed to have at least half a dozen [chickens]. Ducks and geese are also raised. Pigs are a common sight, and dogs and goats roam freely throughout the camp. Because space is at such a premium, there is little room for separate livestock pens. During the day they roam outside and at night they are often brought inside the house (Conquergood, 1988: 188).

This kind of clustering is unheard of in traditional Hmong settlements, which are mostly small hamlets or villages with around a hundred people (Geddes, 1976: 88). The large population in refugee camps created wider channels of marriage alliances and hence new opportunities for political alliances with larger circles of distant relations. The closeness of camp life also created contacts and a broader sense of being Hmong that carried over into life in the United States. Teenagers often told me of other teens now living all over the United States whom they had met or played with as young children in the refugee camps. Many times, they would spot familiar faces of people they had either seen or lived near in the camps while watching Hmong New Year's video film footage taken at various locations throughout the United States.

When I tried to get people to describe what they meant by the camps being noisy they would simply say "too many people." During fieldwork in Ban Vinai, Conquergood describes the visual, olfactory, and auditory soundscape as "an embarrassment of riches in terms of its cultural performance." He writes:

> No matter where you go in the camp, at almost any hour of the day or night, you can simultaneously hear two or three performances, from simple storytelling and folksinging to the elaborate collective ritual performances for the dead that orchestrate multiple media, including drumming, stylized lamentation, ritual chanting, manipulation of funerary artifacts, incense, fire, dancing, and animal sacrifice. Nearly every morning I was awakened before dawn by the drumming and ecstatic chanting of performing shamans. During the day women everywhere would sew *pa ndau* (flower cloth), an intricate textile art that sometimes takes the form of embroidered story quilts with pictorial narratives drawn from history and folklore. Performance permeates the fabric of everyday life in Ban Vinai (Conquergood, 1988: 176).

The Hmong themselves describe these activities not as performance but as ways to bring back into control a social and spiritual world of chaos, a world haunted by sickness, death, and loss. Many sounds that Conquergood describes are the sounds of death and mourning—sounds that the Hmong have described to me as "too noisy, too crowded." The symbolism of these sounds evokes unsettling memories. One woman mentioned to me that she always feels a terror in her stomach when she hears the large funeral drum being played. She tells me "I can't really describe it to you, but I feel cold all over, very cold whenever I hear it." Others talked of headaches that always come over them when they hear the chanting and crying at funeral rituals.

A few Hmong look back on their refugee camp days more positively. Chao lived in Ban Vinai refugee camp for most of his childhood. He got married there and started his family in the camps before emigrating to the United States in the early 1990s. Chao was given a job as a lab technician and translator at the camp hospital. With his salary he was able to have a garden and buy necessities that many had to do without. Although Chao spoke in depth about the many problems of camp life—overcrowding, disease, air pollution from the cooking fires, inadequate sanitation, and malnutrition—he also looked back on his experiences there with nostalgia.

Having lived in the camps for almost fifteen years, Chao felt that before he left he had to have something to remind himself of camp life. During his last two weeks in the camp, he borrowed a camcorder and documented his daily routine. The video shows his living arrangements, his family cooking, and his trip with his two children in his wheelbarrow to his garden and to the well for water. Interspersed with his personal daily routine is the routine of camp life, the long waiting lines for food and water, the bathing facilities, the lines in front of the toilets, and the general layout of the camp. The video is valuable to Chao as a future reference to his past. He made the video for his children, saying "I do not want to forget, and I want them [my children] to remember also."

## EARLY RESETTLEMENT EXPERIENCES

The next major phase in the refugee experience is departure from a refugee camp. Where a refugee goes after leaving a refugee camp is largely determined by the international community and the political climate of the time, the contacts that sending countries have with potential receiving countries, and state policies toward emigration and immigration (Loescher and Scanlan, 1986).

There are three classic possibilities or "durable solutions" for resolving the refugee situation. Refugees can go home, either through voluntary or forced repatriation. They can be allowed to stay in the country to which they fled (called the country of first asylum), or they can be resettled in yet a third country that is willing to give them asylum. These three choices present an increasing order of difficulty for the refugee.

> Going home involved only the most minor cultural adjustment problems although the longer gone the greater the difficulties. The flight to asylum is normally across the nearest friendly border, where the host may be different but not completely strange or unknown. Resettlement, on the other hand, often thousands of miles from home, means leaving not only one's native culture but its wider zone of influence (Stein, 1981: 324).

For the Hmong, returning home was not a viable option; Laos was judged to be unsafe for their return. Thailand also adamantly refused to admit permanently the Hmong or any other Indochinese refugees. Thailand agreed only to house them in refugee camps if the United States and other Western countries took the responsibility for their resettlement outside the region.

The United States' policy towards Indochinese refugees reflected a mix of humanitarian and political motives. The media portrayed these refugees, especially the Boat people, as victims of an "Asian Holocaust," thus evoking memories of the Jewish Holocaust. As Loescher and Scanlan note, "the memory of America's failure to help the Jews in the 1930s was instrumental in the demands made in Congress to resettle Indochinese refugees" and to not repeat the history of the holocaust (1986: 141; see Wyman, 1968 and 1984 on U.S. policy to admitting Jewish refugees in the 1930s).

More important were political considerations. Over the last four decades U.S. foreign policy has been to accept refugees fleeing communist-controlled countries (as exemplified by the Hungarians of 1956 and the Cubans in 1960 and 1966), while at the same time to maintain a closed door policy for refugees fleeing persecution from authoritarian regimes (such as Salvadorians and Haitians). Accepting Indochinese refugees again sent a clear message about how the United States felt about communism.

Hmong refugees were often ambivalent about being resettled in the United States. Kang, a fifty-seven year-old Hmong man, lived in the camps for two years before deciding to come to America. The decision, he explained, was hard:

> In the camps we heard lots of stories about America. There was lots of money here. But we also heard that there was the *pib nyam*, a monster creature with long teeth like the shape of bananas. He was big and tall and eats people and flesh. We laugh now about this. But our relatives still in the camps are not laughing because they have heard about this Jeffrey Dahmer man, and they think he is the *pib nyam*. He killed those boys and ate them. They are scared to come to America for that reason.

Other Hmong still in the camps are frightened by stories from resettled relatives about the difficulty of living in the United States. Through letters and cassette tapes, they hear about how hard it is to learn English and get jobs. They hear horror tales of crime, gangs and drugs. Many prefer to wait in the camps until it is safe to return to Laos rather than face the hardships their U.S. relatives are going through.

The ambivalence of resettlement is complicated by cultural factors as well. One Hmong man in his late twenties desperately wanted to go to America but was held back by his own family. As the oldest son he was required to take care of his parents until one of his younger brothers got married.

The initial period of resettlement in the United States is, understandably, difficult. Hmong refugees recall the confusion they felt in the first few months in this country. They could not communicate their needs, and they had to rethink their habits and routines to deal with a multitude of new situations. One man explained:

> There were so many roads and cars. We needed someone to take us everywhere, to the store, to our house. We were afraid that if we got lost we would not be able to tell anybody anything because we couldn't speak English.

Another man tells of similar problems in his first few months: "We would go to the store and didn't even know what to do or how much to pay for the food. We would just hold out the money and let the people take the right amount."

The confusion and disorientation of resettlement can bring about feelings of nostalgia, depression, anxiety, guilt, anger and frustration in individuals during their first year (Stein, 1981: 325); some may remain embittered and alienated for the rest of their life. There are cases where women and children have become victims of abuse and violence because a spouse or parent was unable to cope with a loss of status or a changed situation. Many older people suffer from homesickness and an inability to make connections to the new culture. In come cases, resettlement has destroyed marriages and family life. One woman in her early fifties talked about how her husband's experiences as a soldier in Laos affected her life in the United States:

> My husband doesn't work now. He was a soldier in Laos in 1972. He got wounded in the head. Three soldiers were there with him when a hand grenade hit all three of them. The other two died and he got a piece of metal in his head. He is crazy now. Very mean. He gets SSI disability.... He was never the same man again. He was always afraid people were coming to kill him. And now he can't even see out of one of his eyes. We separated for two years, and now I divorced him because he was always threatening to kill me.

Another problem that many encountered during their first few months in the United States involved difficulties with their sponsors. The inability to communicate with sponsors created many cultural misunderstandings. One of the first families to arrive in Wausau, the Thaos, related how their sponsor gave them food and then left. As the food dwindled, the family became worried:

It was very hard for our family. No one knew English and there were no Hmong interpreters like there are today. We had no way of asking our sponsors for things. We didn't understand how to get food or even how to go to the grocery store. Our family brought rice with us from Thailand. As the rice was getting low, we didn't know how we were going to get more so we packed up and started walking down the road in search of food. We were finally picked up and brought back. We laugh now about this.

In general, embarrassing and humiliating situations permeated every facet of day-to-day lives for new arrivals. "I was seventeen years old when I came over," a man now in his thirties remembers, "Our family settled in Wausau. At the time [in 1976], there were no ESL classes in Wausau. I was taken and put in elementary school, second grade. I was put in a class with all these little kids. I felt very embarrassed. I learned English real fast to get out of there and then left school and got a job. I went back later and got my GED."

The Wausau school system in the 1970s was unprepared to handle students who were culturally different, lacked education in their home country, and could not speak the English language. Now, the same man says, "The schools understand. There are programs to help our children learn English. Older students are not put in with younger ones, and bilingual aides are there to help the Hmong students."

Still, cultural gaps make the initial adaptation process difficult for many children. One woman, now twenty-seven years old told me:

When I was in high school, a boy in my class sent our family a Christmas card. I kinda liked him and wanted to send his family a card too. But I had no idea where you get these cards. I just didn't know. I am so embarrassed now thinking about it. I ended up cutting his card out and gluing it to a piece of paper and sending it back to him. I can't imagine what his family thought of us.

Another woman who recently graduated from college regrets that she started school in the United States in ninth grade. "It was hard," she said. "I had to just pick up where all the other students were at. To this day I feel like there are things I don't know very well. For instance I never got to learn my animals or colors. I'm always afraid I'm going to get it wrong."

A twenty-seven year-old Hmong man had arrived in Madison two weeks prior to my interview with him. He had lived in Ban Vinai refugee camp for sixteen years, and married and started his family there. His English was excellent and he was excited about starting a new life in the United States. He told me that he didn't want to be like other Hmong who were still on welfare after ten years in the United States. He wanted to get a job right away. The Hmong families who were helping him at the time found his attitude admirable, and told him that he was lucky coming to the United States now rather than when they did ten and fifteen years ago. They reminded him that there are now many Hmong people here to show him things and help him learn. This made the man feel uneasy, saying "My only regrets are that I did not come sooner to America." In fact, many new arrivals feel guilty for not being a part of the beginning resettlement experiences of the group and for having an easier time now that there is an established ethnic community and bilingual interpreters.

Many families tell and retell stories that show how naive and ignorant they were of the new culture when they first arrived. They speak of the linguistic and social blunders that they made and the cultural competence they have now attained (compare with Kirshenblatt-Gimblett, 1983: 40). For instance, one Hmong man spoke with humor of his first night in the United States:

> Our sponsor brought us to our apartment and then left. Someone must have bumped into the thermostat. The house started getting very hot and we didn't know why. We opened all the doors and windows trying to stay cool but nothing helped. We had no idea that the houses could be heated like this and we had no one to tell us what to do. We just sat there roasting until our sponsor came back the next day.

Other families were confused by appliances, not knowing how to work the stove or oven, or by the canned foods their sponsors gave them. Sponsors, who did not realize there would be differences in culture or food preferences, bought their families such food items as canned spaggetti, chili, white bread, and sometimes a small box of Minute rice. Most Hmong families did not know what these foods were or even how to prepare them. One man laughed while telling me "We heard that Americans have dogs and feed them food in the cans. We saw it on TV. So we think, maybe this food is dog food and are scared to try it." Other families were shocked by their first sight of snow. "The snow was very frightening to us" one woman recalled her first few nights in Wisconsin. "It came one night while we were sleeping. We didn't hear it, but when we got up everything outside was white and we couldn't figure out what had happened. We were not sure if it would melt and go away or if this would stay now forever. We even thought that maybe the world was about to end."

As more and more Hmong have become sponsors for their own relatives, cultural mishaps and misunderstandings have become less frequent. There is a limit, however, to what even relatives can do to help new arrivals. For instance, one man who had been in the United States less than six months received a large, official-looking letter in the mail. It had his name printed in large letters and was marked "important":

> At the time I had no idea what this was. I could not read English. I was afraid to even open it. I called my cousin who knows English and he told me he could come and take a look at it that evening. But I worried all day, thinking maybe the American government changed their mind and wanted to send me back to Thailand. I called some more relatives and finally got my uncle's son to come to my house. I am embarrassed now to tell you. The letter was just junk mail. I saved it anyway.

It is not uncommon for Hmong to interpret the initial resettlement experience with cultural symbols from Hmong cosmology and spirit world. To alleviate new arrivals' fears, some Hmong tell their relatives that the spirits that they knew in Thailand and Laos cannot exist in the United States because the many electric lights will scare them off. However, many of the children I met translated experiences in their new environment in terms of the spirit world, combining the descriptions of ghosts and spirits of the folktales their parents told them with popular culture images, such as Teenage Mutant Ninja Turtles.[3]

## CONCLUSION

Comparing Hmong refugees' narratives about escape from Laos with those about entering the United States, it is tempting to conclude that arriving in a safe haven brings about closure to the earlier tragedies of escape. Like literary or historical narratives, we expect a beginning, middle, and end. What we find instead is that personal narratives of escape live on into the resettlement experience; for some, memories of the past color the very outcome of resettlement, while for others the memories are a backdrop against which new difficulties in resettlement are played out.

Memories of war continue to haunt many Hmong today, robbing them of sleep, and tormenting them with nightmares. One man told me: "Sometimes when I am at work, someone will drop a box or something big, making a sound almost like a bomb going off. I jump in fright. The sound reminds me of the war in Laos."

The narratives of Hmong refugee experiences that are told affect Hmong children who may not even have lived in Laos or Thailand. A five year old boy, Kue, started to tell me about his experience in Ban Vinai when his mother interrupted him, saying "Kue, you weren't even born yet. You've never been to Thailand." A six year old girl born in the United States whispered to me one day as an elderly Hmong man passed by her house, "He cries in his sleep at night just like a baby. Everyone can hear him." When I asked her why he cries, she responded that "he is sad and scared of the ghosts in America." Now there are new nightmares to contend with as well. A sixteen year old girl told me that her "father woke up screaming in his sleep last night." When I asked why, she said, "He was dreaming about the gangs and was afraid that my brother might get involved in them."

The memories of life in Laos are easily triggered by sound recordings, photographs, videos, and food from the homeland. One elderly Hmong man's use of a cassette tape recording of birds and animal sounds from Thailand helped ease his homesickness. He told me that putting the tape on in the evening made him feel happy and helped him fall asleep. This same tape, however, was played for a woman in her late fifties. When she heard it she broke down crying. She said the tape reminded her of her daughter's death because "the birds [on the tape] sing like that in August, the month my daughter died in childbirth."

Refugee suffering goes beyond the pain of losing family and country. As Marjorie Muecke notes, "it is deepened by awareness that former cultural solutions, the blueprints for action and interpretation of the world that one learned from childhood, cannot be trusted" (1987: 275).

As the Hmong make new lives for themselves in the United States they are, in many ways, pioneers. People who have lost their homes and homelands, and have suffered through war and trauma, still go on with their lives. Amidst the hardships there are also the joys and excitement of starting new lives.

In the chapters that follow I shift away from themes of tragedy, loss, and initial adjustment to focus on the business of every day life in Hmong households and communities. I examine issues of self-sufficiency and how the Hmong go about making a living, and how they draw on their ethnic community for economic and social support and for maintaining shared traditions and customs. Within the contexts of these day-to-day activities, Hmong narratives are examined for what they can tell us about a people's sense of place and what it means to be Hmong in the United States.

## NOTES

1. Hmong high school students in the St. Paul-Minneapolis area presented the first stage performance of Hmong history and escape from Laos in 1991 in a play entitled "Hmong Tapestries: Voices from the Cloth."

2. See Lynellyn D. Long (1993) on Ban Vinai refugee camp in Thailand where the majority of Hmong were sent after escaping Laos.

3. For a description of Hmong cosmology and the various spirits which roam in the human world see Charles Johnson (1985).

# 3

# Family Life

"**K**aab Npauj [Jo Ann], come on over to eat with us tonight" Mai said to me excitedly when I answered the phone. I recognized her voice. Hmong people rarely identify themselves on the phone. "What time?" I ask. "Right now," she said and hung up.

Mai C., a woman in her early thirties, lived two blocks from my house and was one of my principal informants in Wausau. It is not uncommon to receive last minute invitations from Hmong families. When I arrived she and her husband, Tou, were preparing dinner for a family get-together. By 7:30 over twenty-five people had arrived, including Tou's two uncles (his father's eldest brothers), their wives and children, Tou's sister and her husband, and several of Tou's married cousins and their wives and children.

Mai, Tou, and one of his male cousins worked in the kitchen preparing the food while the family sat in the living room watching Hmong made videos. Mai had boiled eight chickens and the men were cutting them up and preparing a special red meat dish (*nqaib liab*) with hot peppers.

The chicken pieces were placed in a hugh metal bowl in the center of the table along with large bowls of rice, cooked green vegetables, and a bowl of chicken broth. Soda was stacked on one side of the table and paper plates and plastic forks on the other. When Mai called out "Let's eat," the men lined up first to fill their plates, the women and children following. The men and children returned to the living room to eat their meal in front of the television. The women ate around the dining room table and chatted about their children's upcoming parent-teacher conference. Mai translated the letter that her aunt had given her about the school conference.

After dinner Tou played the rented video, *Home Alone*, for his family. The eldest man and his wife did not know how to speak

English but that did not seem to interfere with their enjoyment of the video's action-packed drama. Every so often, an older boy translated parts of the video for his father. The main commentary about the video was not about how the little boy outsmarted the robbers but about how American parents could leave a child home alone. They would never do that, they said. There are always people around in a Hmong home.

The family gathering broke up around 11:00 P.M. Most in the family had jobs or school to go to the next day. Before leaving, both uncles were given foil-wrapped packages of chicken to take home and Mai made arrangements to take her elderly aunt to her doctor's appointment the next day.

The gathering at Mai's house is typical for Hmong families in Wausau and elsewhere. The family is commonly used as a unit of analysis in anthropological studies to detail the realities of human life and the flow of everyday events. As the primary emotional and social center for the Hmong, the family provides security, a place for learning and sharing, and a sense of identification and belonging for its members.

## KINSHIP

Clan and kinship ties are the bases of Hmong culture. They reflect social, political, economic, and historical alliances of families through marriage. The maintenance of these alliances is a necessary part of the adaptation process in the United States. Where a family chooses to live, when they will buy a car or a home, where they will send their children to school, how they will confront an illness, all of these issues fall under the decision-making powers of families and their extended kinship network.

Hmong social organization and family life are based on an extended clan (*xeem*) and lineage (*caj ces*) system which is patriarchal, patrilineal, and patrilocal (Dunnigan, 1982). (Patrilineal descent traces descent exclusively through the male line for purposes of group membership; in a patrilocal residence, a woman goes to live with her husband and his kin at marriage.) Marriage is the creative principle which links clans and individuals. To the Hmong, marriage means having a family and also having good relationships with the other clans (K. Vang, 1982: 44). Marriage is seen as an inevitable part of a person's life course and the only appropriate route for women and men (T. Thao, 1986: 77).

Children provide the continuing link to future alliances with other clan groups and a strengthening of one's own group (Dunnigan, 1982: 127; K. Vang, 1982: 44). Children are seen as future security; they will provide for Hmong families in old age and continue the duties and obligations to the ancestors. Unmarried men and women or childless couples are seen as unfortunate, and homosexuality is claimed to be neither heard of nor practiced in Hmong culture (T. Thao, 1986: 77; Bernatzik, 1947/1970: 128).

There are about twenty different clans in Hmong culture, and representatives of thirteen reside in the Wausau area. Clans are further divided into sub-clans or lineages, in which members trace descent through the male line to a common historical ancestor five or more generations back (Tapp, 1989).

In symbolic terms, the Hmong conceive of the links to their ancestors as their origins or roots; sons are considered the roots of the family, especially as families branch off into separate lineages within the patrilineal clan line. Daughters, on the other hand, do not carry the weight of the past. They will marry out and bear children for other patrilineal clans. They are symbolically part of the present, the "flowers" which "seed" future generations (Tapp, 1989: 158).

Lineage groups are further divided into sub-lineages (*pawg neeg*), in which male heads of household in nuclear families have close agnatic ties with one another and share paternal grandparents. The *pawg neeg* is considered the largest kinship unit capable of collective action. The *pawg neeg* can include anywhere from two to ten households or more (Vang, 1979). Members of these groups traditionally live together in a village or in clusters of nearby villages. Ritual and social responsibilities are carried out by these extended family groups, and, in order to maintain the activities of traditional life, material and human resources are shared. Each sub-lineage group is headed by a group leader with cooperation and consensus from the various households it incorporates (Dunnigan, 1982). The family gathering at Mai's house was part of her husband's sub-lineage. Some of the other relatives not present at the party live in St. Paul and Milwaukee.

Finally, Hmong social structure is further subdivided into the household (*tsev neeg*) which is the most important social and economic unit. The *tsev neeg* represents an "extended family," including a man, his wife or wives, and his sons and their wives and children. The term "household" must be treated rather loosely since it can refer to members living in another house but who come under the authority of the primary householder, as may be the case when different wives, widows, or married sons and their families are living nearby (Barney, 1980: 23).

Each individual is immersed in a web of kinship connections from the moment of their birth until they die. Kin categories are constantly in flux as women are brought into a household and lineage as wives, as daughters are married out, and as children are born and parents die. Hmong identity is defined in terms of overlapping levels, from the individual and his nuclear family to larger units of household, lineage, and clan. The Hmong further divide themselves into other sub-groupings, the principal ones in the United States being White (*Hmoob Dawb*) and Blue Hmong (*Hmoob Ntsuab* or *Moob Ntsuab*). Distinctions between these two groupings include dialect differences and have been based on the traditional dress worn by women.

Finally, the largest category, that of being "Hmong," is also now in flux. Hmong youth, growing up in the United States, struggle to define themselves in terms of their "Hmongness" and their "American-ness," or are placed into larger ethnic categories such as "Asian American" by their schools and jobs.

The kinship category that has the most impact on a Hmong individual's life on a daily basis is that of the household family, or *tsev neeg*. It is with the extended family that most Hmong share their daily tasks and pleasures. In Laos the household family was a residential unit or cluster, whereas in Wausau, members may be scattered around the city. These scattered residential units are thought of as multiple *homes* for the larger family grouping. A child becomes familiar with many houses as *home*, having the liberty to eat, sleep, and play in multiple places with a wide variety of caretakers. Children grow up in close connection with their cousins. Married women move within the tight circle of their husband's extended family as they socialize together, shop and prepare foods for celebrations and rituals, work their gardens, and provide extended family members with child care services when needed.

In Wausau, members of the household family and sub-lineage work, hunt and fish, study ESL lessons, make joint economic investments, discuss family problems, and socialize and celebrate together. In other words, one's friends are usually one's relatives. I rarely met individuals who had formed strong bonds of friendship outside of their own kinship circles.

Although men have wide circles of contact with men of other clans, their principal relationships are with their brothers and father's brother's children, all of whom are classified as *kwv tij*. The term *kwv tij* literally translates as younger and older brother, and is used to refer to the members of a man's own paternal lineage as opposed to his relatives by marriage (*neej tsa*). *Kwv tij* is also used in a much broader sense to refer to all members of a single clan (*xeem*). In this sense, the term means "brothers" and reflects the potential alliances between all lineages carrying the same clan name. The incest taboo is also applied to this broader term; one can not marry anyone with the same clan name, although it is acceptable and desirable to marry one's maternal or paternal cross-cousins because the relationship is seen as stengthening the family alliance.

Most Hmong families desire to be surrounded by their kin. Individual lives and activities are so intertwined with the family group that it is rare to find a Hmong household living in an area where they do not have other relatives. (This only happens when they are fleeing from obligations or problems in their family or clan).

After initial resettlement in the United States, Hmong families began making a series of secondary migrations to be close to their relatives. Migration to new sites has always been practiced by the Hmong throughout the course of their history. In Laos, they moved when the soil was depleted or in order to avoid illness or disease at a certain location. Sometimes they moved to a new site solely for its auspicious qualities. Each move, however, always aligned them with relatives in another area.

In the United States, the Hmong have maintained similar moving strategies. Here, the moves have been undertaken to solve problems of unemployment, to seek areas with training and educational programs, to avoid places with unfavorable welfare regulations, to avoid community tension and, finally and most importantly, to reunite with family and kin (C. Thao, 1982). One teenage girl explained how her family was reunited in Wausau.

> When we all first came to the U.S. we were scattered everywhere. The families were in Kansas, Iowa, California, Colorado, Texas, St. Paul, and other cities. I can't remember them all. But everyone just got together and decided to settle in Wausau. Now just about everyone is here. The Hmong like it best this way, to have the family all close. We like living close. We spend alot of time at my uncle's

house [*txiv hlob*, her father's oldest brother] on Saturdays and Sundays. Everyone just goes over there and talks and spends the day. My father is the youngest of three brothers who live in town.

In Laos, lineage members commonly clustered within the village, making it possible to share in subsistence activities and maintain ritual responsibilities. In the United States, the strategy of kinship clustering provides for the continuation of many traditional cultural practices, including ritual duties. Kin clustering also provides family and kin with feelings of security and promotes feelings of ethnic identity. Extended family households have a clear advantage over nuclear family units in that members defray the cost of living expenses by sharing rent, utilities, and food.

Hmong families also continue to practice traditional forms of leadership and decision making in the United States. However, leadership positions may now be based on an individual's education and knowledge of American culture, rather than on status as the household's eldest male member. There is another change, too. As Hmong women are gaining education and actively participating as cultural brokers within their communities, they are sometimes becoming household leaders and spokespersons for the community at large.

Leaders at all levels of the lineage and clan system are involved in helping kin find employment, training, and housing, and assist in accumulating capital to buy cars, houses, and to pay for education. The wider network of clan affiliations is mobilized in times of crisis, or when moving, visiting, and traveling. As Nicholas Tapp (1982) has shown, Hmong even make use of telephone directories to locate Hmong clan members who live in other states and countries to continue traditional lineage hospitality on a global scale.

## DAILY LIFE

"Nai get up," I hear Yia gently saying to her oldest daughter. Mrs. Yia B. is usually the first one up in the morning. Most Hmong families rise early. A typical day begins around 6:00 A.M., even for family members who are unemployed.

Yia starts the rice cooking in preparation for the morning breakfast, turns on the television, and then starts some of her household chores. Yia is a short thin woman in her early fifties who is going blind in one eye. She has two children who are already married and six younger children, ranging from two to eighteen years old who are still at home. Yia and her family have been in the United States since 1985.

The children straggle downstairs and into the kitchen to grab a bite of food before breakfast but Yia chases them out and tells them to go watch TV. She fills a bowl with cereal and gives it to her oldest daughter to take into the living room for the other children to nibble on.

Morning breakfast in many Hmong households is around 10:30 A.M. for the elders, umemployed, and non-school age children. Family members who have to leave the house for school or work may snack on leftovers from the previous night's meal (cold rice and meat) or skip breakfast all together. Young school age children enjoy eating the popular cereal Kix.

The traditional morning breakfast is usually large, consisting of rice, boiled meat, a green vegetable or boiled squash, and a condiment like hot pepper sauce. Sometimes boiled chicken and noodles are served as a soup for breakfast. Hmong like to eat what is fresh or in season at the time. If they have gone fishing, then steamed fish may also be presented at the morning meal.

Lunch and dinner are similar to the breakfast menu with rice being the main focus of every meal. In fact, one is called to the table to eat by saying *"Noj mov"* or *"Peb noj mov"* which literally means, "eat rice" or "let's eat rice." Dinner is served anywhere from 6:00 P.M. on. If families eat a late breakfast, lunch may be skipped all together.

On this particular morning Yia was preparing extra food because she was expecting a visit from her daughter and son-in-law who live in Minneapolis. Yia's husband, Pao B., came downstairs around 6:30 dressed, as usual, in a good pair of slacks and white shirt. After making a few phone calls to his brothers across town he began tidying up the living room area. Pao is also in his fifties. He used to be an elementary school teacher in Laos before the war. Now he suffers with health problems and receives Supplemental Security Income (SSI) disability. Although he does not work, Pao usually leaves the house about 9:00 A.M. every morning to visit at his brother's house and attend the ESL classes held at one of the local churches. In the afternoons Pao is kept busy running errands, studying English, or fixing cars. Pao's relatives are always dropping by with their cars to ask him for advice. He is known for his mechanical and troubleshooting abilities.

A young Hmong woman preparing breakfast for her family.

Unlike her husband, Yia hardly ever leaves the house because of her young children. She doesn't like to take them with her because it is too much of a nuisance, especially in the winter when they have to be bundled up. The city does not require Yia to attend ESL classes because she has a child at home under three years old. But Yia's life is not isolated. Female relatives constantly stop by. Most of her in-laws visit her house on a daily basis. During the winter months, the women usually bring their small children in the mornings or afternoons and spend the whole day talking, watching videos, cooking, and playing with the children. Yia occasionally babysits for her relatives if they have to go to the store or to a doctor's appointment. But she does not make a practice of this. Her relatives never leave their children with Yia for more than a couple of hours.

Like other Hmong women, Yia's female relatives occasionally spend the afternoon trying on their Hmong New Year's clothing. These occasions are festive and full of laughter as the women spend hours helping each other get into their various sets of skirts so that they can take photographs of themselves.

In the house next to Yia's lives a woman name Pang G. Although it appears that she is a single mother with six children, she is in fact the second wife (*niam yaum*) in a polygynous relationship. Pang's husband, Va B., lives across town with his first wife, who is related to Va as a cousin and is a member of his clan group.

Pang is a frequent visitor at Yia's house and a constant companion because of their kinship ties. They visit, cook, and eat together, share in childcare duties, and go to the store and work their cucumber fields together. Because Yia is unable to drive, Pang takes her to the store whenever she needs to go. The two women usually go once a month to purchase a whole pig at a farm outside of Green Bay and then come home and split the meat between their two families.

Va is a frequent visitor at Pang's house during the day. He picks up the children and takes them to school and runs errands for them. He sleeps at Pang's house every other night. Neither Pang, Va, nor Va's first wife work. They have been in the United States for five years now and all receive Aid to Families with Dependent Children (AFDC).[1]

Pang is also on the go, often visiting her husband's first wife and leaving her oldest daughter, Vue, in charge of the children while she is gone. Va is trying to find Pang an apartment closer to his. In the meantime, Pang depends on seven-year old Vue to babysit while she goes to the store and the gardens. Vue cooks and does other household chores as well. Vue knows that if anything happens she is to run next door to Yia's house. In fact, the children are often at Yia's house playing while Pang is away.

Although Pang is unusual in her long absences away from her young children, it is not unusual for families to assign childcare and household duties to pre-teen and teenage daughters. Exactly when daughters start to become "little mothers" varies, mainly depending on the household's composition. If no older female relatives are around, then daughters are pressed into service to help their mothers at a young age.

In an extended family household, grandparents assume many childcare duties. Often, a woman's mother or mother-in-law becomes the principal caregiver, especially when the husband and wife have full-time jobs. Sometimes, families draw on relatives in different cities to help out. I knew of two households in which the

grandmother was shared by her married sons in Madison and Seattle. She resided permanently in Madison with her husband and
her youngest son's family. However, when her older son's wife
had a baby, she flew to Seattle and stayed for six months to help
tend to the household chores and the new baby. Her husband,
meanwhile, stayed in Madison to assume the childcare duties for
his youngest son while his son and daugther-in-law worked.

When the family is not an extended one, household and child
care duties usually fall to the mother and her daughters. I met one
eight-year old girl who was staying with her grandmother for the
summer while her parents worked in the cucumber fields. She
told me she liked going to her grandmother's house because her
grandmother does not make her cook. "Oh, I've been cooking
since I was five years old." She told me:

> I get up at five in the morning and fix the rice and get
> breakfast ready for my parents who have to be at work at
> seven o'clock. Then I go back to sleep for a little bit until
> my sisters wake me up for school. My older sisters can't
> get up as early as I do so that is why my mother lets me
> cook. Then she makes them cook on the weekends.

Her parents liked to take a warm breakfast to work with them
and eat it at work during their lunch break. One other family I
met had assigned their six year old daughter the duty of getting
the younger children ready for bed. Each night she gave her three
brothers their baths and put clean clothes on them.

In the summertime many women work in the cucumber or
ginseng fields (see Chapter 5). During this time many childcare
duties are done by unemployed male household members, teenagers out of school, and grandparents or other household members unable to work.

It is not uncommon to see Hmong men cooking or doing
household chores. Consider the case of one family in the F clan.
Mr. F, now in his mid-fifties, was injured during the war and cannot see clearly. He is unable to drive because of his disability. He
relies heavily on his wife to take him places. She does most of the
shopping and errands. In return, Mr. F has assumed many of the
household chores and the cooking, although his teenage children
also help out after school and on weekends.

Men also cook after their wife has given birth to a child. After
childbirth, a woman is not supposed to do any cooking or house-

work for one month according to traditional Hmong customs. A new mother is required to follow a prescribed diet of eating only chicken and rice. It is also taboo for her to touch or eat anything considered cold; violating this taboo can cause sickness or complications for a woman later in life. If she does not have a mother-in-law or mother staying with her to help, then household duties fall to the husband. In fact, many of these customs are not strictly followed in Wausau due to the conflicts they cause when men are employed and have difficulty assuming all the household duties.

Most men also prepare foods for rituals and ceremonies, cutting and chopping meats in preparation for their wives to cook. Men cook when their wives are sick or away at their gardens for the day. I have also observed men cooking for enjoyment. One teenage boy I met cooked all the family meals without any ridicule from family or friends about this being "female work." A Hmong man in the Madison area learned to cook by taking a job in a Japanese restaurant. "I worked at the Japanese restaurant Ginza," he explained:

> The Japanese are very strict. They only show you how to do something once and then you are on your own. It was very hard working there at first because I didn't know anything and couldn't get it by just seeing it once. The main head cook was a Hmong man who told me 'I show you only once.' I said to him,'Hey, wait a minute. Are you Hmong or are you Japanese? If you are Hmong you will show me at least three times. Not just one.' I told the Hmong man to think about it. I gave him half an hour to answer me. The Hmong man decided he was Hmong and would try to teach me everything he knew. I had to convince him that if he ever got sick or in an accident, then I would have to know everything about the job or else the restaurant would close down. After that, things went pretty good. Actually, I started to learn more and more about cooking by watching TV. I watched those shows that showed the cooking lessons. This is where I got my ideas for cooking in the Japanese restaurant. I would just try new things at the restaurant from the TV and the boss would ask me, 'Where you learn this? It's good.' But I wouldn't tell him. I think a person can learn a lot from TV.

Even though the sexual division of labor of household chores is blurred in many Hmong families, the roles of mother and father are more clear-cut, especially when children are past infancy. At an early age, children are cared for by both mother and father. It is just as common to see the father assisting in feeding, changing diapers, and carrying the infant in a baby carrier on his back as it is to see the mother doing these activities. In fact, some of my most memorable early experiences with the Hmong were in watching fathers coddle and dote over their infant children.

After the child reaches three or four years old, the mother becomes the predominant figure in ordering the child's home life with chores and errands. Most children and teens can talk freely to their mothers but not to their fathers. Fathers are seen as authoritarian. Mothers are the nurturers. Several teens told me that if they wanted to tell their father something important, such as what was happening to them at school or to relay their thoughts on career or marriage, they went to their mother first. She, in turn, would tell their father in order to bring the issue to the forefront. Once in the open, the father might bring other members of his household together to discuss the matter.

When teenagers need money they go to their mother. They do not have to plead with her. Rather, they simply tell her what the money is needed for. In the cases I observed, mothers usually went to their purse and gave the teens the money without further questions asked. I rarely saw mothers quarrel with their children over the money or suggest how it should be spent. The mother holds the purse strings in most of the families that I came to know. It was part of their role to budget the family's finances. Several women told me that they also held money for their husband. As one woman put it "I give him an allowance and we save the rest," referring to the money from her husband's paycheck.

Hmong family finances, in general, are discussed openly around children; at quite early ages they know the monetary value of houses, cars, rental properties, and other living expenses. In several families I met, boys as young as three and four years old were included in their family's decisions to buy a new vehicle.

Family cooperation is stressed in all activities. From an early age children learn their roles and obligations for helping their family, be it household chores, childcare duties, or the good study habits needed to get a good job in the future. The attitude is that each family member works towards the good of the family. The burden of this responsibility for teenagers, especially those who are struggling to be "American," has caused tension with their parents. In most cases, the parental generation is confused, angry, and unsure of how to handle their teenage children. Teens are counted on to make something of their lives and are asked to contribute to the needs of their families. They are told to study hard in school, yet they are also expected to devote a great deal of time to being cultural brokers for relatives, by translating letters and bills and interpreting during phone calls and for visitors and appointments. If they fail, the whole family loses face in the community. In one such case, a young man returned home after failing his first year of college. He was given very little freedom thereafter. His father assigned him remedial homework until he felt his son could return to college. The talk around the community was that the young man was lazy and had wasted his parent's money while in college. No one wanted to vouch for him as a worker so that he could get a job, and I was told that none of the local girls would even consider him as a potential marriage partner.

## HMONG HOMES

The first impression one gets while visiting many Hmong homes is that of sparsity and poverty. Many families live in low-rent apartments that are poorly maintained by landlords. Apartment walls are often cracked, dirty, and thinly or sloppily painted. Windows may be broken, shades torn or missing, carpets ragged and stained, and appliances old and worn. Families that rent in low-income areas tolerate these conditions because they fear that complaints may lead to higher rents or eviction notices. Most families do not take it upon themselves to repaint walls or make repairs. Most told me that it was not their property; they had no right to make changes.

The living room is the central room for the family's social life. Household furnishings are generally kept to a minimum and are usually hand-me-downs received from a sponsor or purchased at a second hand store. The essential living room furniture consists of two or three couches, a TV set, and sometimes a coffee table or some other table. The TV set is the main focus in almost every Hmong home. It is usually turned on first thing in the morning and only turned off when the family goes to bed at night. Couches are essential for entertaining the numerous and frequent visitors who are a daily part of Hmong life. Sometimes families can have as many as a hundred visitors, especially if they are holding a special ritual or ceremonial event. In these situations, folding chairs are borrowed from relatives in order to seat all the guests.

There are usually few if any decorations or knick-knacks in the living room. If one finds knick-knacks, they are usually located near the TV area, resting on either a purchased entertainment center or some other makeshift stand for the TV. The walls in the room are usually bare;lighting comes from a single ceiling lamp. If there are pictures hanging on the walls, they are usually of relatives and ancestors or the school pictures of the children, and they are placed high on the wall out of reach of small children. An occasional calendar or poster with an Asian theme or landscape, such as mountains, rivers, forests, animals or tourists spots, may also be taped to the walls for decoration. Colorful straw mats from Thailand decorate the floor and hide the worn carpeting in many homes.

Bedrooms also contain the barest essentials. Beds are either with or without bed frames. Not many families bother buying chest of drawers or other bedroom furnishings. Clothes are usually stored in cardboard boxes or plastic laundry baskets. If the family consists of small children, the mattresses are sometimes pushed together, making one gigantic bed so that the children have the security of being in the same bedroom with their parents. Hmong parents find it odd that most people in the United States insist on putting their children into separate rooms to sleep alone.

The bedrooms are used solely for sleeping and getting dressed. Children never play in their bedrooms and, if they nap, they usually do so on a couch in the living room or on the mat on the floor. Although many teenagers decorate their bedrooms with the latest popular culture posters, they do not spend time in their bedrooms either. Most teens do their homework on the couch, at the kitchen table, or at the local library.

Even the newborn baby's space is in the living room. There is no crib tucked away in some quiet corner. From the moment of birth the baby sleeps surrounded by the noisy and bustling environment of the living room. When the baby is awake, family members are constantly centered around the baby, doling out kisses, or touching, hugging, cooing and jostling the baby. A need for private space does not seem to be an issue in Hmong households. Most activities are done in the company of the family. As such, homework and problem solving become a group effort rather than a chore for a single individual.

Some non-Hmong residents of Wausau have commented to me that the Hmong seem to like living this way, referring to the rundown apartments and the lack of material goods. Their comments imply that the Hmong must not know any better. In fact, as soon as families can afford to, they move into better maintained apartments or buy their own home and try to create a more aesthetic and pleasing environment in the house. Families usually buy new couches after they purchase a home, and look for furnishings that are of higher quality than the used furniture they were given when they first arrived.

Many Hmong families are frugal and selective about how they wish to spend their money. They do not want to initially invest their money in new household items like couches and other furnishings if they can get them free or at a reasonable price. Decorative furnishings such as lamps, tables, drapes, art works and other items are unimportant to them when their primary goals are to save and get ahead—and when other consumer goods have higher priority.

## CONSUMER GOODS AND CONSUMPTION BEHAVIOR

Household goods and furnishings in a Hmong home vary according to the amount of time that a family has been in the United States and/or the economic and job opportunities that they have had. Despite economic differences, however, there are similarities in the way all Hmong families utilize the space in their homes and decide what to save for and how best to spend their money. In regards to saving and finances, Mrs. Chia A warned me that the Hmong would not be open with me on this issue,

> Savings are a very private matter. They [welfare families] know that they are supposed to use all the welfare completely up. So they may be afraid to tell you that they are saving. But saving comes first with the Hmong. Then they pay the bills, and the last thing is always money for food. They always save first. The parents decide together exactly how much money they will save and how much is needed for the budget and the food. They might not want to give you a true account. They will probably tell you they do not have anything.

After a family arrives in America, relatives help them to furnish their apartment the best they can. From that point on, however, the family begins saving for its main purchase, an automobile. Without an automobile the family is totally dependent on relatives for everything—getting rides to ESL classes, to grocery stores, laundry mats, jobs, and school.

Many non-Hmong residents in Wausau become angered by the sight of Hmong people driving new model cars. The automobile is a symbol of wealth, status, and freedom in the United States. Many non-Hmong residents feel that the Hmong are not yet entitled to own brand-new cars, especially if they are on welfare. Upon being accused by a neighbor of being a "welfare cheat," one Hmong woman explained to me: "We need a car just as much as any other American, and why not buy one that is dependable and large enough to carry our whole family. Besides, these things are on the market for anyone to buy. What does it matter to these Americans what we buy? We don't question how they spend their money." Indeed, many Hmong families forfeit buying a new couch and other luxuries of middle class life in order to save for a car.

Relatives who work may initially help with the car purchase by establishing credit and getting a bank car loan. What happens is that the family gives the employed relative the initial down payment to purchase the car. The working relative holds the title with the understanding that his relatives will make the monthly payments and pay for the auto insurance. Although on paper the car is owned by the working relative, a verbal agreement exists which reflects the actual ownership.

Extension of credit to lineage members expands beyond the local community. Those who work may have relatives all over the United States whom they help financially. For instance, Mr. Xa C and his wife Xai both had jobs in local Wausau factories. When I met them they had been in the United States a little over three years and had just purchased a duplex. Besides the mortgage on their house, Mr. C also held the titles to two vehicles in California which his nephew and cousin were paying him for. He said he had another cousin in St. Paul who was looking for a car as well.

Extension of credit to relatives is common for other purchases as well. The fact is that a system of verbal agreements works to channel credit throughout the kinship system, providing opportunities for relatives to buy things that they might not otherwise be able to purchase through normal credit channels.

Ultimately I found that many of the families on welfare saved because they feared hard times. One woman on welfare, with six children and a disabled husband, expressed her feelings of insecurity about the welfare system: "We save money back because we worry that the government will one day just decide they do not want to help refugees anymore. What will we do then? How will we eat and pay our bills? How can we get jobs when my husband cannot work. This is why we are careful."

Most families present themselves as modest and frugal. Diets and lifestyles are kept simple. Items like rice and wholesale meats are purchased in bulk at extremely low prices compared to supermarket prices. Many staple foods such as rice, noodles, fish sauce and various seasonings are purchased at local ethnic food stores. Many families in the Wausau area also prefer to purchase a whole cow or pig and live chickens. Pork is purchased from a local farm ouside of Green Bay. The farmer sells a live pig and then butchers it. On the average, a whole pig costs between $100 to $140. The meat is brought home, divided up among kin, and packaged for the freezer. The bones are used to make soup bases, and the skin is cooked down into oil for frying.

A considerable amount of money is also saved because most Hmong do not smoke, drink alcohol or consume coffee or tea. I was reminded of this one day when a Hmong man wanted to know why most people in the United States could not save money. When I told him I didn't really know the reason, he proceeded to tell me: "You Americans don't have money because you get paid on Friday and go drink it up. I know. I see my neighbors. They do this. Every Friday night they go to the bar and drink."

Even a family's everyday clothing is modest. There seems to be no need for showy fashions except among teenagers; parents usually buy them the latest styles for the school year so that they can fit in with other teens. Meanwhile the parents continue to wear basic clothing purchased at discount or secondhand stores or from yard sales.

A large part of the Hmong family's social life and entertainment centers around family and home and engaging in activities that do not cost money. Eating out or going to the movies are usually avoided by new immigrant families. Family entertainment takes place in parks, involves playing volleyball and soccer with relatives or watching a rented video at home. Weekends are used to travel to nearby Hmong communities to visit with relatives.

Only recently have Hmong families begun taking vacations, and even then they may arrange their vacations so that they stay with relatives rather than pay the cost of a motel. One family was so thrifty that they refused to pay the two dollar entrance fee for parking to attend the annual Hmong Fourth of July soccer games held in St. Paul. While food booths were set up throughout the park selling Hmong foods, the family spent the night before preparing foods to be eaten during the day's outing. Many Hmong families also carry food with them in the car when they travel in order to avoid the expense of having to stop and eat at a restaurant. It is not uncommon to see a family stopped by a roadside park, eating rice and chicken prepared especially for the trip.

Many parents want their children to have more material goods than they have, and are willing therefore, to scrimp and save for the future. This prudent lifestyle, however, presents tension and conflict with young teens trying to fit into American culture. Many teenagers told me that they never invited their non-Hmong school friends over to the house. Only a few teens were brave enough to tell me the reason. Having been to their American friends' houses, they felt embarrassed by the things that their family owned, the old furniture and the look of the apartment.

Maintaining impressive displays of wealth in the form of expensive living and dining room furniture is of no concern to many Hmong families, I am told, because they do not want to incite jealousy among their Hmong neighbors and relatives. Wealth is manifested in other types of material goods, such as a woman's Hmong New Year's costumes, gold and silver jewelry, and other traditional possessions, valued for the statements they make to the Hmong community rather than to the non-Hmong community.

The Hmong participate in the U.S. consumer market, but their consumption behavior is selective. The majority of Hmong families find it important to own a television, a VCR, a cassette recorder, a camera, a rice cooker, and a freezer. Some families also own stereo systems, camcorders, and microwave ovens. Buying a television set allows the Hmong a lens through which to view U.S. life and gives them a feeling of participation in it—if only through entertainment. At the same time, modern goods reinforce ethnic identity and relations. Videocassette recorders, for example, give the Hmong a means of watching videos in their own language, and hence the opportunity to create their own community and reaffirm their ethnic identity. Camcorders, cassette recorders, and cameras facilitate communications between families at a distance, and aid in maintaining traditional kinship connections.

A commonplace item, the freezer, has an important symbolic—as well as practical—importance to the Hmong. Most Hmong families try to purchase a freezer within their first year in the United States. The freezer signifies the household's ability to save and provide for itself and the family. Beyond food storage, a freezer (or freezers) symbolizes the social resources of kinship, kindness, reciprocity, labor, and self-sufficiency, and serves as an identifying marker, distinguishing the difference between Hmong and other U.S. groups. The freezer maintains the social realm of family and kinship ties by facilitating the process of food storage and food sharing. It provides the link of food for socializing, for maintaining the family's health and its well-being and sense of economic security. Seen in the light of Hmong cultural adjustment and adaptation to the United States, the freezer allows the Hmong to maintain traditional cultural values and practices as well as providing them with an economic edge in a consumer and cash-based society.

Most Hmong families did not feel the need to buy a washer and dryer even though they spent exhorbitant amounts of money each week at the laundromat. Although I pointed out to several families that they could buy a washer and dryer three times over with the amount of money being spent at the laundromat, their remarks to me were usually "We don't need these things." One family told me: "we're saving for another freezer instead."

These remarks may seem odd and contradictory at first, especially coming from a people who are frugal and careful with money and who look for ways to cut expenses. But consumer decisions are not always based on financial motives. Many Hmong rent apartments, making it inconvenient to own washers and dryers. Furthermore, laundromats have become places where Hmong can go to socialize and gossip with other Hmong. Laundromats provide Hmong women with a "legitimate" place for getting out of the house to meet and talk with other Hmong women. A Hmong college student who is from California informed me that many laundromats in California are now equipped with VCRs, providing Hmong clientele with the opportunity to wash their clothes while also watching Hmong-made videos in a larger social group setting.

Once the car and other major appliances are purchased there is a continued practice of thrift and saving for a home or to send children to college. In fact, one man I met said he had already started saving for his three sons' college education. His sons at the time were six, four, and two years old.

## EDUCATIONAL GOALS AND ASPIRATIONS

Most Hmong families recognize that the only way their children will succeed in the United States is to get an education. The majority of Hmong, as noted in earlier chapters, have immigrated with little or no education, training, or job skills. Some parents fear that they will not be able to provide their children with appropriate knowledge and educational experiences needed for growing up in the United States. For instance, a man in his early forties, who has been in America for twelve years, worries about the cultural gap that his own children will feel:

> I do not take my family out to restaurants. I cannot afford it. My children, they will be ignorant of this. American parents always take their children to restaurants. But my children, they won't know anything, not how to order from a menu or how to eat at the table. Who will teach them these things? The school does not teach these things.

Limiting educational experiences because of thrift was a concern of some families. A Hmong man working at the Hmong Association told me that there are Hmong families that are too thrifty, never doing anything with their children outside the home, never letting them go anywhere or join extra-curricular activities at school because they do not want to incur any expenses. He felt that this may hurt the child's educational opportunities in the long run.

More typically, parents are beginning to buy their children computers for school, video games for recreation, and are paying for them to go on school field trips. In fact many families that I talked with are planning their children's college education while their children are still in grade school. Besides the financial planning, parents are also providing encouragement and direction by suggesting possible careers and goals.

One night while I was visiting Chia's family, I overheard the conversation that she and her eight year old daughter were having. Chia's husband was in his second year of college and had just bought a computer to help in his course work. I had been invited up to the family's bedroom to examine the new computer. Chia's husband, her two older sons and I were gathered around the computer while Chia and her daughter sat on the bed. Chia's daughter asked her mother, "Mommy am I going to go to college like daddy?" Chia answered her daughter, "Yes dear you are." She then proceeded to tell her daughter how her future life story would unfold:

> First you will go on to high school and graduate and get your papers. Then you will go to college and study and get a job and work a little too. And then you will get married and have a couple of children. And then you will go back to college and graduate, and get your papers. And then you will get your job.

Another woman, in her late twenties expressed similar thoughts. She was taking classes in book-keeping and accounting at the local technical college. The day I interviewed her, her son (age 4) and daughter (age 2) were in the living room playing school. I asked her: "What do you want for your children?" She answered that she wasn't quite sure yet:

> For my daughter, I want her to finish school, and if she has talent [I want her] to go on to higher schooling. My husband tells her she should go to college and be a nurse. And he tells my little boy to go to college and be a doctor. Already my little girl, she's two and she puts on her backpack and tells me she is going to school now. She's just pretending, but she wants to go. They made a new law now that three year olds will be able to go to pre-school. That is good. I want her to go.

These kinds of remarks were not just confined to the younger families nor to families already working in the job market. Several elderly men in their sixties expressed their desire for their grandchildren to become well educated. One of these men told me that he had been a shaman and a salesman in Laos and knew how to make many things with his hands. He saw education as being at the root of everything:

> I want my sons and daughters to use their brains to get money. Don't use the muscles to work. I want them to go get education. They can have all the animals and land but

no education. It is only the education that will give things
to them.

Hmong national conferences are now held annually around
the country, including Wisconsin, in order to encourage and inform parents and students about the value and importance of education. In addition, the different clans have organized their own
clan educational conferences. A man from the *Her* clan told me
that his group meets annually in Colorado and that everyone tries
to come. He told me: "We are telling our children that they must
go to school and get their degrees. They must go to college and get
their master's degrees. We know that we can not be anything in
this country without degrees."

While many parents are encouraging their children to seek
higher education as a means for bettering their lives in the United
States, they continue to practice strategies learned in the home
country for providing for their families. I examine the issue of
Hmong economic activities and attitudes and behaviors towards
work and achieving self-sufficiency in the next three chapters.

## NOTES

1. At the time of my study, the State of Wisconsin granted benefits for unemployed parents under the AFDC program called
   AFDC-UP. I address this further in Chapter 5.

# 4

# Community

Tong was leaning over a large loom, untangling some of the threads when I walked into the Neighbor's Place, an old building in the heart of one of the Hmong neighborhoods. Tong looked up from what she was doing to greet me. Boisterously she said in broken English "I make this rug," and then continued with the shuddle to weave the cloth through the loom. Tong, who is fifty-five years old, comes to the center three afternoons a week with about fifteen other Hmong women for ESL lessons. She always comes early so that she can work on her rug.

The other women started arriving around 3:30, pulling out chairs and setting up the makeshift classroom. The atmosphere is informal and noisy. Women bring their children with them. While they take their language lesson, their children play in the adjoining room where there is a kitchen, a piano, tables, and boxes of toys. Interruptions are constant as children run back and forth from the play area to their mothers. Many of the women who attend these afternoon classes have been at home all day. This is their first opportunity to get out of the house. Like Tong, they look forward to meeting with the other women.

After class I drove Tong home. As I started up the hill on 10TH Avenue towards her apartment, Tong broke into song, singing "Amazing Grace" in Hmong. At first I was surprised and then delighted by her relaxed mood and willingness to sing in front of me. Tong is in the Hmong church choir and wanted to show me what they were learning. She carried the tune in a traditional Hmong style by raising her voice and then letting it quiver at the highest note before sliding back down to the low ones.

"Teach me the words Tong," I said excitedly, "so we can sing together." All the way home we rehearsed the first stanza in Hmong and she promised to teach me the rest of the song when she learned it better. When I arrived at her apartment, her cousin was already waiting to take her to the church for her choir meeting.

## THE ETHNIC COMMUNITY

When we think of immigrant groups coming to the United States, clustered in ethnic ghettos, we usually imagine them socializing because they share a language, culture and customs. What I found among the Hmong was that socializing was a family, not an ethnic, matter—confined to relatives rather than neighbors. All of the families that I have mentioned so far were next-door neighbors; only those who were related visited together. Yia B., for example, was frequently in her backyard garden but she never even greeted or talked with Mee J. or Chue F., who were just next door.

The women attending the ESL classes at the Neighbor's Place all lived close by, some on the same street or within several blocks of one another. During classes, the women were cordial and seemed to enjoy one another's company. Yet after class hours, the women rarely had contact with one another unless they were related. They did not visit each other's homes and did not know each other's phone numbers.

This situation was made clearer to me one day when an emergency arose. A young women named Cha J. from the ESL class called me one morning early to ask for my help. Her baby had become feverish and needed to be hospitalized. She and her husband needed someone to look after their three small children for about an hour while they admitted the baby to the hospital. They asked me to go with them to the hospital. When I inquired about who was going to watch the children, Cha remarked that they were still trying to contact her husband's relatives. When I suggested that perhaps they could leave the children with her next door neighbor, Xai E., the woman that Cha always sat next to in English class, Cha adamantly said "No, they are too busy to be bothered."

Instead of asking a Hmong neighbor for help, people go to relatives, even if it is inconvenient and they live far away. One reason Hmong households try to rent apartments close to relatives is to make life easier. Children can run back and forth to their relatives' homes, and relatives are nearby to help.

The automobile is important in bridging the spatial gap between relatives. It is also important for women to learn to drive. Women who cannot drive or have not yet obtained a driver's license are extremely isolated within the ethnic community, especially if their relatives do not live within walking distance. A woman who does not drive is dependent on her husband to do many of the household errands and shopping while she stays home to care for the children. Once a woman learns to drive, however, her husband watches the children while she goes shopping or to the gardens.

Groups that extend beyond kinship networks do come together during special public events such as Hmong New Year's celebrations or during the summer on men's soccer and volleyball teams. Yet, even in public places the Hmong tend to segregate by lineage and clans. Marathon County Park in the summertime, with a crowd of Hmong socializing in the back area, may appear to outsiders as a large family get-together. What we find within the large group of Hmong, however, are pockets of families; the Yang in one area, the Vang, Thao, and Her in another area, with little interaction between the groups. Activity as well as identity are primarily grounded in one's own lineage group first and then only secondarily in the larger Hmong community.

But isolation in one's own kin group does not mean that families are not aware of larger community events or that a sense of community does not exist. One of the main organizations that fosters a sense of community among the Hmong is the Wausau Area Hmong Mutual Association. The Hmong Association offers a variety of programs and services to the Southeast Asian community. They include job information, development, training and placement services (discussed in Chapter 5), health-care education, family counseling, housing, school services, programs for youths, women and the elderly, and citizenship preparation.

One of the main functions of the Hmong Mutual Association has been to provide cultural transition services to the refugee community. Educational services include everything from medical assistance, translation and interpreter services and school liason programs to general information on culturally appropriate behavior in U.S. culture. Information is disseminated by a quarterly Hmong Newsletter printed in both Hmong and English, a weekly one-hour Hmong radio broadcast, and through scheduled programs on various topics. Advertisements from car dealers, funeral homes, banks, and other businesses that sponsor the one hour radio program on Sunday mornings suggest some of the ways that the Hmong connect to the non-Hmong world.

Recent articles in the newsletters have included pieces on how to keep your house clean, parenting skills, pregnancy and vaccinations, dealing with loneliness, and planning and budgeting money. Seminars on such topics as buying a home, filing income taxes, preparing children for educational success, and home maintenance are a few of the offerings held for the immigrants of Wausau.

A variety of weekly classes are also offered. Hmong culture and language classes are held twice a week for school-age children, and citizenship preparation classes are held for adults. The "Good Friend's Club" was also formed to offer fellowship opportunities and cultural education to the elderly Hmong. Association-sponsored field trips and other activities help reduce the isolation and loneliness that many elderly Hmong people have experienced in their new cultural setting. The Progress-Asian Youth (PAY) program was initiated to provide counselling to youth and their parents as well as organize social activities and tutoring to help young people for whom delinquency is a risk.

Programs targeted at Hmong women have dealt with everything from safety in the home to issues of how to understand hospital procedures and children's education. A women's support group, Hope, was initiated by a group of college-bound women to discuss issues of marriage and work, women's rights in Hmong culture, and the changing roles and attitudes of Hmong women in the United States.

Other programs in the Wausau area besides the Hmong Mutual Association have contributed to a Hmong sense of community and fellowship. The various adult ESL classes held weekdays at various local churches and at the Neighbor's Place (funded by the United Way and church donations) have brought Hmong and other refugee people together for language and cultural learning and provided a new avenue for socializing. For example, the Neighbor's Place serves as an outlet for local gossip, women's trading of goods (such as sewing, thread, vegetables), providing services (massage, babysitting), and exchanging knowledge regarding illness, and herbal and folk remedies. The classes at the Neighbor's Place have given Hmong women a chance to meet with many non-Hmong neighbors, go on fieldtrips, and learn about various U.S. holidays, traditions, and activities, such as food preparation, sewing, weaving, and music.

Although socializing did not seem to extend beyond the classroom, the skills that were learned were often tried and tested in the home. Women wanted to know how to prepare some of the foods that their children were eating in the school cafeteria. Their young children would come home requesting Jello or pudding but the women had no idea what these foods were or where to find them at in the grocery store. Many times ESL lessons at the Neighbor's Place combined information about products and their use with the daily language lesson of identifying the product in the store and how to read the words on the box.

Some women had also gone to their children's music concerts and wanted to learn the songs. Since I knew how to play the piano I decided to teach them several simple folk melodies, one being "Are you Sleeping?" The women enjoyed this so much that several commented later that they could not get the melodies out of their mind, or that the singing lesson helped them understand what their children were doing in school.

The Hmong Christian and Missionary Alliance Church provided fellowship not only on Sundays but also throughout the week with regular Wednesday night prayer meetings, women's and men's discussion groups, youth and adult choirs, and periodic church activities that coincided with U.S. holidays and traditions. Most of the planning and cooking for the church events like Easter, Christmas, Mother's and Father's Day, and church picnics fell to the women's church group. The Hmong church also set up food booths and stalls selling embroidered story cloth pieces (*paj ntaub*) at various local non-Hmong community events to raise money for the church.

A sense of community is also maintained by the four Hmong ethnic food stores in Wausau. These stores are gathering places for Hmong men and women. Besides providing traditional food items like bulk rice and imported noodles, vegetables, and canned goods from Thailand, the stores sell many non-food items as well. Clothing, pots and pans, dishes, floor mats, and the latest video and cassettes are just some of the items sold. One of the main ethnic food stores in Wausau also provides a meeting ground in the basement of the store where men can play pool and talk. Store bulletin boards post everything from general announcements to job openings, apartment rentals, and homes and cars for sale. Most of the stores also extend credit to regular customers in the form of a running tally payable at the end of the month.

## HEALTH CARE

When the Hmong greet each other they say "Are you eating tasty, staying well?" ("*Koj puas noj kab, nyob zoo*"). In symbolic terms, the greeting reflects two main concerns in Hmong culture: health and illness.

According to Hmong cosmology, the human body consists of a number of souls which work together in a harmonious relationship. When the body's life souls get out of harmony, then illness can occur. If any one of the body's numerous souls become separated or lost then the result may be disease and death. The Hmong believe that everything in the natural world such as trees, animals, rivers, and caves also contains a spirit or soul. Furthermore, there are evil spirits that live on earth and ancestral spirits or the souls of the dead which continue to interact with the living. Like the spirits in the natural world, ancestral and evil spirits can cause illness, especially if an individual has violated a taboo or has been careless in his or her actions.

Disharmony in the body and subsequent illness can be brought on by a host of factors such as eating the wrong foods, overworking, excessive worry, sadness, and natural causes such as old age. Treatment of physical symptoms utilizes herbal remedies, massage, and diet. Illness caused by soul loss or by other spirits requires the assistance of a shaman. The shaman (*txiv neeb* or father of spirits) is able to travel to the supernatural realm and communicate with the spirits either by negotiation or battle.

A major source of confusion and conflict for the Hmong has been in the realm of western medical health care practices. Many western practices are in direct conflict with Hmong traditional beliefs and practices. Some aspects of western medicine are perceived by the Hmong as a strange mixture of technological and surgical procedures with mystifying medical jargon.[1] Surgery and the drawing of blood are feared as potential causes of soul loss. Immunization shots have confused parents, especially when they have caused a healthy child to suddenly become ill. Bacteria, viruses, and germs are relatively new concepts to most Hmong. Nearly every Hmong family has a story to tell about their experiences with western medicial treatment. These medical narratives in many ways parallel the narratives of escape by focusing on the element of tragedy and the inability to have control over the situation.

Women have felt the most vulnerable to cultural misunderstanding in their dealings with doctors and hospitals, especially during prenatal care and in the birthing process. Pelvic exams are considered to be embarrassing and done in excess; and postpartum checkups are thought of as just another way for doctors to make money. The birth process in the hospital is viewed as noisy, busy, and uncomfortable. After having three children in Laos, one woman recalled:

> My first child born in America was a very bad experience for me. They tied me down, my legs and hands, so that I could not move. I had no energy or strength in this position to push the baby.... I didn't speak English so I could not get anyone to help me or listen to me. I refuse to go back to the hospital again. I had three more children since then but I delivered them myself in my own house. My husband didn't even help me. One child even came out with the [umbilical] cord around his neck, but this did not scare me like the hospital.

The Hmong community in Wausau supports a number of traditional specialists in the area of health maintenance and healing. Shamans, herbalists, and masseuses are actively supported in conjunction with western medical treatments. The Hmong healers provide a bridge between traditional practices and modern biomedical treatments.

## The Shaman

Most families who need a shaman's services usually utilize the shaman within their own clan. This means that the shaman travels to their homes to perform healing ceremonies (*ua neeb*) or to call back a lost soul (*hu plig*). Shamans can be either male or female. I knew several male shaman in the Wausau area who were continually gone from their residence on the weekends, traveling to various cities in Wisconsin and to the St.Paul-Minneapolis area to perform healing ceremonies for their relatives. The services provided by the women shaman I met were more localized and rarely included long distance traveling.

Most healing ceremonies in the United States are now held on the weekends to accommodate the schedules of working rela-

Shamanistic ritual being held for a sick relative. The shaman is in the background. In the foreground, her helper is preparing and offering spirit money.

tives. The ceremony is an all day affair and relatives from all over the commuting area are requested to attend. Immediate relatives locate and purchase a live pig and chickens in preparation for the sacrifical part of the ceremony. The shaman goes into trance and "shake" sometimes up to four hours. During this time, the shaman pleads with the spirits to take the soul of the animal in return for the individual's soul. The ceremonies can become quite noisy with the beating of a large gong and the chanting and stomping of the shaman during trance. There have been cases in Wausau where non-Hmong neighbors have called the police to complain about the noise.

After the animal is sacrificed, the meat is cooked and served to all the guests in attendance. Soon after everyone has eaten, the guests leave.

Chindarsi's study of the Blue Hmong in Thailand revealed that the Hmong consulted shamans of the same clan because they were then less apt to be charged as much, or the shaman would refuse payment altogether (1976: 45). Payment varies with each case. One male shaman told me that he earned around fifty dollars for each ceremony. He also received some of the meat from the ceremony. At the ceremonies I observed, portions of the meat from the sacrificed animal were always given to the shaman before he or she departed and cash may have been exchanged in private as well. Hmong are not usually required to pay for services until there is positive proof of successful treatment or recovery; otherwise no payment is necessary.

## The Herbalist

Almost every woman grows some herbs (*tshuaj*) in her home and knows how to use some basic herbs for treating colds, fevers, headaches, and menstrual pains. Women gain knowledge of herbal remedies as illnesses in the family arise. If they do not know how to cure the illness themselves, they have the principal responsibility to seek out therapies from other individuals who do know, usually an herbal specialist. Advice and information are often sought first from the extended family network, and then from more distant relatives.

Depending on the nature of the illness, family members rarely like to go outside their kinship channels to receive therapy. For instance, an elderly man was experiencing impotence due to a diabetic condition. His family was too shy to mention this problem to the medical doctor who was prescribing insulin for his diabetes.

I found out about the man's illness accidentally. The man's wife was preparing an herbal remedy for him to take that evening. She put a small hen with some herbs on the stove to cook and then ran off on an errand to her neighbor's house. Shortly after she left I smelled something burning in the house and discovered the pot on the stove. The daughter-in-law felt obligated to tell me what the mixture was for, revealing her father-in-law's problem and asking me if I knew how to solve it. When I asked why they did not go to the herbalist who lived just five houses away, the daughter-in-law told me that they did not want this to be known in the community. Instead, she was seeking advice from her relatives in California and in Thailand.

Other cases which caused a concern for privacy were those relating to sexually transmitted diseases (STD). In two incidents, women were told by their husbands that they had contracted a venereal disease and requested that their wives find a remedy for them. In both cases, the husbands had contracted the disease while on vacation in Thailand. Both wives called those family members closest to them to ask for assistance in finding an herbal remedy. These cases became a concern to me when a group of women were complaining about their husbands' activities while in the homeland.

Hmong men are beginning to return to Thailand during the Hmong New Year celebration, staying for about one month. During this time, some men are reported to stop first in Bangkok to visit the brothels, and then head into the villages to meet eligible young women. Most of the women I met did not understand the danger of HIV or that Bangkok was a high risk city for contracting the HIV virus which leads to AIDS. They felt AIDS was a curable disease and could be treated similarly to syphilis or gonorrhea. When I checked with the local medical and family planning clinics in Wausau to see if Hmong men or women were coming for treatment of sexually transmitted diseases, both places told me, "No." The doctors and nurses at these clinics were unaware of Hmong returning to the homeland or that they were engaging in high risk behavior that could put them at risk for sexually transmitted diseases. Given their resistance to pelvic exams, Hmong women are at further risk for developing complications from sexually transmitted diseases, especially those that present no visible early warning signs or symptoms.

Remedies for female illnesses, especially for infertility and menstrual problems, were the concern of the whole community. Women with these problems were open to suggestion and therapy by people both inside and outside of their kinship circle. Usually women heard about the efficacy of a certain herb or treatment through the success of an individual case.

For instance, Xai J., a widow in her mid-fifties, began experiencing menstrual problems. Refusing to accept the doctor's opinion that she was beginning menopause and had cancer, Xai began telling her problem to the women in her church group and, at the same time, contacting her relatives in Thailand. By the end of six months she had received seeds from the homeland to grow an herb that was supposed to be beneficial for regulating the menstrual cycle. Her problem cleared up and other women began coming to her house to get clippings of the herb to use for similar or related problems, paying Xai if the herb was effective for them as well.

Individuals who have a wide knowledge of various herbs usually are sought out by other clan members and, in more serious cases, non-clan members. Herbal specialists are still popular despite a family's ability to obtain medicines from physicians.

Sometimes a family will seek the help of an herbalist as a last resort or even in conjunction with biomedical treatment, especially if the sick person is a baby or young child. Payment for services is again only made if there has been an improvement or a cure. I was unable to collect data on the amount of payment received by herbalists. I was always told, "They pay me whatever they feel is enough." Most herbalists felt that their services as herbalists were rendered as a duty to ease pain and suffering and not done with a profit motive in mind. In-kind payment is also common practice and made in the form of food or other non-food gifts.

Chinese pharmaceuticals as well as over-the-counter drugs purchased by relatives in Thailand are also sent to families in the United States. Many of these pharmaceutical drugs are packaged with instructions in Thai or Chinese; their utilization is based on word of mouth, previous success stories, and experimentation based on the illustrations on the packaging. One of the boxes had an illustration of a man and woman smiling at each other. These pills, I was told, were "to help with pregnancy."

## The Masseuse

Another service offered in the Hmong community is that of massage (*zuaj*, or *mos ib ce*). There is always someone in the kinship network who knows about massage and how to manipulate parts of the body when a relative or friend is experiencing illness or pain. As with herbal remedies, individuals who practice massage learn through their own experiences of illness. Most women treat headaches by giving neck and shoulder massages. One woman told me that her father-in-law was a specialist in treating stomach pain (*mos plab*). Some individuals learn to treat a variety of ills and become experts in the field. Some become nationally known and travel extensively around the country to give treatment.

One such case is an elderly Hmong man in California who has gained a reputation throughout Hmong communities in the United States for handling female disorders, especially infertility. He claims that one can reposition the womb through massage, making it ready for a baby and hence relieving infertility. His massage technique is also acclaimed for bringing about the desired sex of a baby. Several families I knew either sent their daughter-in-laws out to California to receive treatment from this Hmong specialist or else paid for the masseur's airfare to come to them.

I was fortunate to meet this man when he was flown to Wausau to be thanked and paid for "fixing it" so that a woman could have a girl baby. While he was in Wausau for two weeks, women from all over the community met with him for massage treatment, either for infertility or for the selection of the sex of their next child. He declared that he has brought at least 385 children into the world by his technique; at least these were the ones he has been thanked for.

In the Wausau area, several women had gained local reputations outside their own kinship channels for using massage to cure headaches, stomach aches, muscle pains, and to treat illness due to fright (*txais ceeb*). I found out about these women through my own experiences of illness.

When I mentioned to one family that I had been surprised by a small child who stole up behind me and touched me when I thought I was all alone, they said that I must go immediately to their relative for treatment of my fright. Fright can lead to illness and soul loss. The masseuse was able to see me immediately. She massaged my arms, legs, neck, and head, and used a fresh piece of ginger to run up along the veins of the arms, legs and back. Ginger is used, she said, because its vein-like appearance resembles that of the body's and promotes healing. After she finished, she instructed me to come back the next morning to repeat the massage and again on the following day to complete the therapy. It was necessary, she said, to repeat the procedure three times.

When I asked what I owed her, she told me to pay her whatever I could afford, but only after she finished the therapy and only if I thought it was beneficial. She told me that people pay her between $10 to $30 for a series of three sessions. The sessions can take from twenty minutes to an hour. I found out later that Hmong people in the Wausau area visit this woman for treatment of pain or because their children have been frightened by a dream or a sudden fall or if they have cried or felt agitated without reason. Many times a masseuse will also have knowledge of herbs and combine these two talents in treating illness.

## Role of Magic, Fate, Amulets, and Prayer in Health Care

Incantations and magic (*khawv koob*) are also used to produce a cure and sometimes to cause evil against another person. My only experiences were with magicians who were able to cure. The curing ritual of the magician is not as complex as the shaman's. Formulaic words are said over the person in order to exorcise the evil spirit causing the illness. I first observed this type of magic when I visited a widow suffering from severe depression. Her son-in-law had diagnosed her illness as having been caused by possession by the sun spirit. To counteract the spirit, he applied magical words over a paper figure which he cut out and hung over the kitchen stove. Several other Hmong families said they applied magical words over a knife and then placed it in their window sill to ward off any evil spirits that may be lurking in the night. One Christian Hmong family told me that a Bible placed under one's pillow will have the same effect as the magical knife.

Wearing or possessing charms and amulets can also protect a person from evil or misfortune as well as increase one's good fortune. Charms are usually worn on the wrist or around the neck, and their presence is viewed as an insurance for good health. Amulets are especially visible on newborn babies and small children.

Hmong people also believe in a "mandate of life." The mandate is given to each individual before birth and specifies the length of the person's existence on earth as well as his fate (X. Thao, 1984: 325–26). Hand readers and various other fortune tellers may be able to read the mandate to determine the cause of illness. If illness is one's fate, sometimes an appeal to supernatural forces by a shaman can get the individual an extension to the life already determined by the mandate.

The role of the Hmong Christian and Missionary Alliance Church in the health care process should not be overlooked. They use prayer sessions to bring about a cure. Members of the church meet at a sick person's house and read from the Bible, sing hymns, and ask the sick person and family members to give testimony. During the sessions that I attended, the leading women of the church organized prayer sessions which included a light meal. During the two or so hours that these events lasted, the women used the opportunity to chat with each other, to share stories about their experiences in the United States, and their memories of the homeland, and to update each other on relationships, pregnancies, their children's lives and a host of other issues. The atmosphere was usually festive and lively.

Church members also conduct prayer sessions for Hmong patients at the hospital. When the person recovers from illness they usually hold a "thank you" celebration and invite all those who have helped to affect a cure. One celebration I attended was held in the Hmong church. The family holding the celebration had invited about two hundred guests for a sit-down lunch. Speeches and testimonies were again a part of the ceremony.

Traditional channels of healing can be as costly as a visit to the hospital. The social obligations incurred from an illness can run into hundreds of dollars. The cost is usually absorbed by the members of the household family (*tsev neeg*) and the sub-lineage (*pawg neeg*).

## Death

When death occurs, family members from all over the United States and abroad will be contacted and arrangements made for their arrival. The news of a death spreads very rapidly in the Hmong community. It travels by word of mouth to the close kin and then, by telephone to the rest of the community and beyond. When a Hmong woman in Wausau committed suicide one morning, most of the Hmong knew of her death by noontime. I was informed of the death by a phone call from the victim's distant cousin. She in turn had learned of the death at her ESL class. In another case, an elderly man in Wausau died while I was in Madison. I learned of his death that evening while visiting a Madison Hmong family who were preparing to go to the funeral. They were not related to him but knew him from the refugee camp in Ban Vinai.

Death (*kev mob kev tuag*), for most Hmong, is understood as a journey requiring special rituals and a showing of the way–song (*qhuab ke*) to guide the soul back to the afterworld. The words of the song detail the hazards and dangers of the journey and tell the deceased where to stay before being reincarnated (see Chindarsi, 1976; Tapp, 1989).

A proper funeral is necessary to insure the soul's prosperity in the afterworld. A proper funeral consists of various rituals, including killing an appropriate number of cows in honor of the deceased. In fact, family members will console the dying person by telling them how many cows they will kill. When my neighbor's sixteen year old daughter informed me that her paternal grandmother finally died after a prolonged illness, she said: "My father and my uncles went to the hospital and told my grandmother they would kill at least three cows for her. This made her happy." The three brothers were each obligated to contribute a cow to the funeral to symbolize her importance in the family. The meat from the cows was then used to feed the guests who attended her funeral. The number of cows killed also symbolizes the status and prestige of the individual.

Maintaining traditional rituals of death in the United States is difficult because they are in direct conflict with U.S. legal codes. Adapting to state regulations for the handling of the corpse has meant that Hmong must relinquish some of their traditional mortuary customs such as the washing and handling of the body. Furthermore, Hmong have had to adjust their rituals to the rules and regulations of funeral homes. Instead of holding a wake around the deceased in their home, families are limited to the funeral home's visitation hours. Restrictions on noise at the funeral home have also limited the use of the traditional musical instruments, the drum and the *qeej*, to announce the death and guide the deceased soul back to the afterworld. Even cemeteries are in conflict with traditional burial customs which utilize geomancy and land forms for finding the most auspicious location to bury the deceased—a location which will bring good fortune to the deceased and the male descendants (see Tapp, 1989).

The funeral homes in Wausau have been very accommodating to the Hmong by offering extended visitation hours and allowing them access to the home for some ritual and kinship duties. Helke Funeral Home, the principal funeral home used by the Hmong, has provided special caskets to meet Hmong ritual needs.

Funeral homes are packed to capacity when there is a Hmong death. Relatives and non-relatives from the community attend the visitation. During the visitation, men and women sit segregated on different sides of the room. A relative is commonly seen taping the event with a camcorder to document the people in attendance. At this time photographs of the deceased and the coffin are also taken.

Most Hmong funerals have opened caskets. The deceased may be wearing traditional embroidered burial clothing or western garb. Deceased males tended to be buried in suits, whereas the three deceased females that I observed wore traditional burial clothing.

Guests and family members stand and view the body, some touching it and crying, and speaking words to the deceased such as, "Why do you leave us now?" or "We will miss you so much." Because Hmong language is tonal, some of the dialogue to the deceased sounds like song. During several funerals I attended, family members placed a tape recorder on the lid of the coffin in order to record the mournings of each guest. Women as well as men can be seen crying at funerals. Children are also present and are not restrained from going up to look in the casket on their own.

During the visitation hours, male relatives go around to the funeral guests handing out soda pop as a thank you gift for their attendance. Most people do not open the can; instead, they take it home with them. Periodically, male family members will come into the room where the coffin is and bow down in thanks to members who have contributed towards the burial expenses. In the two Christian Hmong funerals that I attended, a table was set up in the back of the room and men collected money from the various relatives in attendance or from people who owed money to the deceased. It is important that accounts of the deceased are settled so that they can enter the next life debt-free.

At the same time that the visitation is taking place, some female relatives are at the home of the deceased cooking and feeding the numerous guests. For three days or more, feeding the guests is a round the clock activity. The family is required to provide breakfast, lunch and dinner. Funeral food typically consists of boiled beef and rice, and sometimes a peppery sauce dish used as a condiment. Soda and beer are also served.

Relatives and friends will sit up throughout the nights before the burial to comfort the family of the deceased and make sure they do not get lonely. During these wakes, relatives tell stories, sing, joke, and play cards to keep people from getting sad.

All family and kin are required to go to the cemetary on the day of the burial. At the cemetary, the casket may again be opened to check and straighten the position of the body and ready it for its journey. If it is a traditional burial, the ritual specialists (*tus qhaub ke*) will speak once again to the deceased, giving directions to the afterworld, before the casket is closed and lowered into the ground.

All adult male relatives from both the affinal and consanguineal clans form a line and take turns shoveling dirt into the hole until the hole is completely filled. One Hmong man told me: "We do this because we will be asked by others 'Is this person really dead?' and we will be able to say, 'Yes, because we buried him with our own hands.'"

Burial does not end the customary ritual process for many non-Christian Hmong. Numerous rites take place on the thir-

Principal cook preparing food for the funeral guests.

teenth day of death, and then again within a year of the death. Honoring the ancestors properly will insure that their needs will be met in the afterworld, and that they will not bring trouble to the living relatives in the form of illness or social and financial problems.

## HMONG AND NON-HMONG INTERACTION

There seemed to be very little interaction between the Hmong and their "American" neighbors. The "Americans" in the apartment below mine had lived there for five years and had never talked with any of their Hmong neighbors until I arrived. I found that during my research, I had little contact with the non-Hmong population in the Wausau area except at the hospital, doctors' offices, and other social service agencies.

Most Hmong women told me they would like to have American friends but were not sure how to go about it. Several women said that they tried to be friends with their American neighbors by giving them vegetables from their gardens but nothing ever came of it. Another woman who worked in the school system as a bilingual aide had a lot of contact with American women at work, but had never been invited to their homes. Several times when

Americans dropped in on her family during dinnertime, she invited them to stay and eat with the family, but the Americans never did. The Hmong woman asked me: "What are we doing wrong? We really wanted them to eat with us and share our food? What should I say to them to make them stay next time?" An American woman and long time resident of Wausau told me she felt the Hmong were very "clannish" and didn't want American friendship. She told me that she tried to cultivate a friendship with her Hmong neighbors by taking some baked goods to their house one day, but she said, "They never returned the gesture." This angered her and she never made another gesture of goodwill towards the family.

In order to remedy this segregation, one high school teacher started the Pals program which matches a Hmong student with an "Anglo" student. They are then responsible for each other for the school year and do something together, outside of school, at least once a month. Although the program matches individual students, some families have been drawn into the friendship process. When I asked the teacher why more students did not have Hmong friends he replied:

> It is hard for Hmong to make Anglo friends just because, for one thing, if you can't communicate you can't make friends. But there are other factors like cliques and sports groups and all that. You usually make friends with a circle of people you are actively involved with. It is very hard for a Hmong person to be friends with a football player. They just don't move in the same circles. There aren't many overlaps in the social activities of the Hmong and Anglo. And then you take the Hmong women. They don't get involved in sports because of their parents. The parents are concerned for them and they are told to come home and take responsibility for the house and watch the children. Also, probably 50 percent of the women students are already mothers and have obligations at home.

Although Hmong families started moving to Wausau in the late 1970s, there are still many misconceptions and stereotypes about the Hmong. To remedy this, local newspaper articles and educational programs have tried to highlight Hmong culture. But many times the articles are too general and the educational programs do not seem to reach the people who hold the stereotypes.

Many of the stereotypes reflect a trend of anti-immigrant folklore, common at the national level, about the Hmong and other Southeast Asian refugees. Rumors and jokes about Southeast Asian refugees often refer to food. Florence Baer (1982) collected rumors about Vietnamese refugees in California and found that they focused on bizarre eating habits, such as eating stolen pets, while at the same time, ascribing to the group traits like dirtiness, talking "funny", having lots of children, and "sticking together" as part of being foreign and poor. Roger Mitchell's (1987) research in Eau Claire, Wisconsin found similar tales about dog meat sandwiches being eaten by Hmong students and allegations by non-Hmong of having seen freezers full of frozen dogs in Hmong homes. Hmong families confessed to me that they are often harrassed on the phone, sometimes late at night, with obscene phone calls and people asking them if they eat dog meat. In my first few weeks in Wausau I heard rumors from the non-Hmong population about how the Hmong killed and ate all the wild ducks in the area, stole dogs to eat, and roamed the city parks as gangs.

Other incidents of prejudice, discrimination, and racism have occurred in Wausau as well. Children report being called derogatory names at school or picked on in the halls. Hmong teens told about non-Hmong people driving by in their cars who have hurled epithets at them as they walked down the street. A Hmong college-educated woman recalled the time she was walking on the sidewalk to her job when a group of young teenage boys deliberately splashed her by driving through a puddle of muddy water and then drove off laughing.

Hmong families in my neighborhood remember tensions and animosities that they experienced several years ago. Their children were harrassed by neighborhood children and adults when they were outside playing. "It wasn't safe then," Mrs. F's teenage daughter recalls. "They would call us names, throw eggs all over our cars, or throw beer cans at our windows. It's not like that now but we are still careful." They are so careful that many Hmong families do not let their young children play outside, fearful that the children will make too much noise and disturb their non-Hmong neighbors. Many Hmong parents confine their children's play to indoors or to the public parks in the evening. Children are usually very excited to get back to school on Monday, especially if they have spent most of the weekend at home and inside. Overall, many of the Hmong families that I met chose to maintain a low profile even when provoked, in order not to start any trouble. Hmong teens, however, are not as adept at maintaining a stoic face when ridiculed or taunted.

The Hmong face discrimination in the realm of housing. Families wishing to rent an apartment may call the listed ad in the paper only to be told that the apartment is already rented; yet they will continue to see the apartment advertised in the paper for several more weeks. A Hmong neighbor of mine hurried to buy the local newspaper one evening so that she could be the first to call about apartment vacancies. She was told that the apartment was taken. I called the number a few minutes later and was told to come over and take a look at the apartment. The landlady assured me that the apartment was still available. Of course my Hmong friend was hurt. She asked me, "How can they judge me like this when they have not even met me? Do they think they know all about me from my voice?"

Incidents such as these occur frequently enough so that the Hmong Mutual Association intervenes for Hmong families having difficulty renting an apartment. A non-Hmong worker at the association makes the phone calls to prospective landlords so as not to reveal the identity of the interested renters.

The tension between the Hmong and non-Hmong population in Wausau is not solely racially motivated. The rapid influx of Hmong to Wausau has had a tremendous impact on the city's resources. High Hmong birth rates have caused increased enrollments in local elementary schools. The Wausau School District's property tax rate rose to 10.48 percent in 1993, a figure that was three times higher than the other districts (Pfaff, 1995: 76–77). Taxes in themselves were not the only issues fueling anti-immigrant sentiment. Many Hmong were clustered in neighborhoods where housing was less expensive, thus their children created a majority at a few of the elementary schools. For instance, in 1992, 62 percent of the student enrollment at Wausau's Lincoln Elementary School was Hmong (Pfaff, 1995: 77).

Many Hmong children do not learn English until they begin public school. Non-Hmong parents fear that their own children's education will suffer because so much attention is being given to enculturating Hmong students. For their part, Hmong parents feel that if their children are in the majority in a school they may not be adequately exposed to U.S. culture. One solution to this dilemma was a proposed busing plan which would distribute

Hmong and non-Hmong students more evenly throughout the district. This plan was finally implemented in September of 1993, but not without great debate.

Welfare receipt by the Hmong has been a primary element fueling inter-ethnic tension within the Wausau community. Welfare reform in Wisconsin starting in 1996 has recently moved more Hmong families from welfare to work, thus dropping the welfare dependency rate to about 40 percent as of 1997. Many of these families are now working at minimum wage jobs. However, it is too early to tell what the full effects of the welfare reform will be on the Hmong, and indeed on Wisconsin's poor population in general.

## NOTES

1. Although medical misunderstanding has been a major problem, Wausau has initiated a program where Hmong interpreters are now trained in medical terminology and procedures in order to better inform the Hmong individuals and their families. Even so, there are still many cultural mishaps. One film by Fink and Yang (1983) attempts to address this issue for the non-Hmong and medical community.

# 5

# **W**ork and Ethnic Enterprises

**O**ne morning, on my way to Zoua's house, a small boy called out to me from his front porch. It was Peter H. I knew him from the Neighbor's Place. Although his mother never came to the center's ESL classes, he did, mainly to play with the toys at the day care center while his cousins were learning English.

"Kab Npauj, my father wants you to come visit us," Peter shouted to me.

When I entered the house, Peter's father was sitting in the living room looking out the window. He was a tall man in his late forties wearing a white shirt and black slacks. I knew from other Hmong women that his family was large, with eleven children in all. Peter was his second to youngest son.

"You've come," Mr. Vang H said to me as I entered the front door and removed my shoes.

"I've come," I answered back, wondering why he wanted to talk with me. He told me that he knew I was visiting with the Hmong families. He was wondering when I was ever going to make it over to his house for a visit. I apologized for not dropping by sooner. With this said, Mr. H began to tell me his life story.

"I came to America ten years ago," he stated firmly. His wife peaked out from the kitchen, smiling. "You've come." She too seemed delighted. She was preparing the morning breakfast. I knew I would be invited to eat with them. She was a plump, healthy-looking woman in her early thirties. Her youngest child, a four month old baby, was asleep on her back in a baby carrier. She wiped the sweat from her forehead and then returned to the kitchen. I could hear her chopping the meat and vegetables for the meal.

Without a second thought, Mr. H continued:

"We got married in 1971 when everything in Laos was no good because of the war."

"Were you a soldier?" I asked.

"No, I was a construction worker. I worked with the government and the United States. I helped build dams for irrigation. I worked on eight different dams. I also built houses and bridges."

"What do you do for work now, in Wausau?" I asked.

"Nothing," he answered and then continued to explain what he meant. "What can I do? I have been here ten years and cannot get a job. I mean I cannot get a job that pays any money to feed my family. Every job in America wants a person to have a certificate of some kind to prove they can do the job. They do not have the time to just see if the person can already do the work. This is not important. They want the certificate. No one will hire me. All I can do is give my family money for the food. This is all we have. This is all that any of us Hmong people can give to our families."

"Does your wife work?" I asked sheepishly.

"No, she doesn't work. She has the children to take care of."

"Does she have a vegetable or pickle garden?" I ask out of curiosity.

"Oh, yes, she has. This she has."

## UNEMPLOYMENT, WELFARE, AND SELF-SUFFICIENCY

The primary U.S. policy–concerns in the Indochinese resettlement process were their adjustment and capacity to achieve economic self-sufficiency. The Refugee Act of 1980 mandated annual surveys and reports to Congress in order to measure the progress and success of refugees coming to the U.S. Information about employment and the use of social services were the two main categories used for accessing refugee adaptation and self-sufficiency (Gordon, 1989: 24).

The Office of Refugee Resettlement funded studies specifically focused on Hmong resettlement. These studies were conducted in seven key locations between the fall of 1982 and the spring of 1983, using interviewing and group meetings. The goal was to determine what the resettlment experience has been like for the Hmong in the various locations and how they have been faring in terms of employment, welfare dependence, and adjustment. The studies examined areas of employment, economic strategies used by the Hmong, the communities affected by Hmong resettlement, and employment projects that proved successful for the Hmong. They also investigated impediments to successful resettlement and self-sufficiency, a major one being English language acquisition. Issues of education, the future of Hmong youth, and the role of secondary migration were also highlighted.[1]

The conclusions reached were that in states where welfare benefits were minimal, dependency rates and unemployment rates were considerably lower for the Hmong. States which had generous welfare benefits had high Hmong dependency and higher unemployment. Independence from welfare was higher among refugees who had been in the country longer.

Labor force participation was influenced by age, gender, education, and English language speaking–ability. The majority of the Hmong in the United States are under age fifteen (49%) with 25% of this total under five. Another 4–5% of the population is over sixty. The studies found that most people forty-five years and older were unemployed due to their age, health, or inability to learn English. A large majority between the ages of sixteen and thirty-four were unemployed because they were in school or pursuing some kind of training.

The studies concluded that women were less likely to be employed than men, due to family responsibilities and childcare duties. Women also arrived in the United States less equipped for labor force participation; unlike the Hmong men, women had little opportunity in their own country for schooling or second language learning. However, as noted in Chapter 3, in the early years of resettlement men may share a good many childcare responsibilities and this may limit their labor participation as well as women's (Bach and Carroll-Seguin, 1986: 398–9).

Sponsorship has been a key factor in immigrant and refugee participation in the labor force. There are five types of sponsorship available to emigrants and refugees: by an individual U.S.

citizen, family, church group, voluntary agency, or refugee's relative. In the Wausau area, most Hmong were sponsored through
the Lutheran Immigration and Refugee Service (LIRS) or the
United States Catholic Conference (USCC).

More Hmong in the United States are starting to sponsor their
relatives. Ethnic sponsorship can reduce feelings of anxiety and
stress for the new arrival. However, in terms of employment opportunities, it has been argued that "sponsorship by a member or
organization representing the host society might be able to provide refugees more opportunities to make a better integration
than sponsorship by their own ethnic group" (Tran, 1991: 541). In
fact, Bach and Carroll-Seguin note that refugees participating in
the labor force are significantly more likely to have been resettled
by a U.S. family, and those out of the labor force are more likely to
have been sponsored by a relative or agency (1986: 394).

My own research suggests that it's not that ethnic sponsors
lacked knowledge or insight into employment opportunities.
Rather, ethnic sponsors imparted a general attitude that welfare
receipt was a normal and expected part of the first few years of resettlement in order to take advantage of the ESL classes and training programs before attempting work. Often, the choice is to
delay employment in order to gain skills and training with the
hopes of entering the labor force at a higher rate of pay.

Ethnic sponsors, knowledgeable about social and welfare programs like SSI disability and aged benefits, encouraged their relatives to apply for these benefits. One Hmong woman who was
relatively well-informed about the SSI program had a continual
stream of relatives from Milwaukee and Minnesota coming to live
with her temporarily, so that she could help them in the disability
application process. Most Hmong who were receiving SSI did not
considered it as a form of welfare, but as a resource that they
might use, especially if they felt they could not work.

I found that many Hmong had a clear idea of the job market
and the wages being paid at various factories. For some, the decision to delay entering the job market was an unwillingness to
take just any job. Many people had unrealistic expectations about
being able to hold out for a job that paid $8.00 to $9.00 an hour,
even though they had no prior work experience outside of farm
labor, and limited English language skills. Realistically, most figured out that a job paying anything less than this made staying on
welfare advantageous, especially given that they could get family

medical coverage through Medicaid on AFDC. Indeed, a Wisconsin Legislative Fiscal Bureau study concluded that a parent on welfare would have more total income than a non-welfare parent making $8.00 an hour ("It Pays to Stay on Welfare," 1993).

The Hmong I talked with believe that most Americans have high-paying jobs and earn well over $9.00 an hour. This view is reinforced by the kind of people involved in a helping capacity with the Hmong; most volunteers, sponsors, and other agency personnel are in middle-income brackets and their homes and cars reflect this. Further reinforcement of the image that most people in the United States have good-paying jobs comes from television, the main way many Hmong get an inside view of the American family home. Rarely did the Hmong families I interviewed have opportunities to visit the homes of their non-Hmong neighbors to make comparisons with the television image.

Quite a few of the Hmong families who were employed and off welfare complained to me that their non-Hmong sponsors had abandoned them, no longer coming to visit or check up on them. For most Hmong, this was disheartening because they saw the relationship as a sort of patronship, and expected to maintain a lifelong contact with their U.S. sponsor.

As of 1988, the Hmong made up approximately 2.2% of the monthly caseload of all 86,000 families receiving AFDC in the State of Wisconsin. Furthermore, 18–20% of these families received benefits under the state's program for unemployed parents (AFDC-UP). This program provided benefits to households with two unemployed parents in order to discourage men from abandoning families so their wives could qualify for AFDC. In 1988 1,900 or 90% of the 2,080 Hmong families receiving AFDC in Wisconsin received AFDC-UP benefits. However, by 1990, the number of Hmong families receiving AFDC actually dropped by 10% to 1885 families despite the addition of over 600 new Hmong families in the state (Fass, 1991: 20).

Although about half of all Hmong in Wausau were receiving welfare at the time of this study in 1990, the fear that this will create a permanent cycle of poverty is clearly unfounded in light of the educational success of Hmong children. Fass notes that Hmong student grades are "usually 40% higher than for native Wisconsin students, the high school dropout rate is negligible, the graduation rate is close to 100%, and the share of graduates going on to technical school and college is also very high" (1991: 2). In fact, in the Wausau area, over 90% of Hmong students compared to 40% of non-Hmong students are continuing education beyond high school. Fass correctly points out:

> If this standard of performance sustains itself, self-sufficiency of the vast majority of the next generation of Hmong adults seems almost guaranteed. Hmong children on welfare today seem to have every likelihood of taking their parents off of welfare tomorrow (1991: 2).

Overall, resettlement and self-sufficiency studies have concluded that an assessment of Hmong economic adjustment needs to take into account factors other than just employment status. Employment is an individual matter, whereas self-sufficiency extends beyond the individual to the kin-based group and the household.

The Hmong household is the unit of production for self-sufficiency and for consumption. The extended household provides the mechanism by which the Hmong can pool economic resources from both wage and non-wage sources and thus improve their level of economic well-being. As Robert Bach notes "the size and composition of the extended household enlarge the household collective wage fund" and "also increase access to state assistance" (1988: 47). One household member may have a job, another may be on AFDC, and there can be several wage earners or welfare recipients as well. Taking the household as the unit of analysis, welfare use may be a strategy to increase the household's income—and not signify dependency at all.

## EMPLOYMENT IN WAUSAU

On the whole, government studies in Wisconsin and elsewhere show that the Hmong have low-level and low-paying jobs. Many have entry-level, light, manufacturing positions which require minimal English skills, such as in electronic assembly, machine operation, jewelry grinding, sorting and collating, and food processing. Others are employed in minimum wage agricultural jobs, nursery work, janitorial and food services positions. Some have been able to get semi-skilled jobs because of their prior experience in Laos in fields like metal fabrication, carpentry work, and industrial sewing. Jobs requiring vocational training, such as machinists, welders, tool and die makers, are limited to individuals with higher levels of English proficiency. Bilingual social-service jobs with schools, hospitals, mutual aid associations and other social services have opened up for the few Hmong with bilingual and bicultural skills. Finally, some Hmong men and women have found positions as seasonal farm laborers.

In Wausau, many of the Hmong with low-level job and English language skills are employed in factory work. Men have found jobs in the lumber and building materials industry, manufacturing plywoods, windows, and doors. Other men work in the local cheese-processing plants or in light manufacturing jobs.

Mee's husband, Mr. E, worked at the plywood plant for $7.00 an hour. Mee was able to get a part-time job with the Hmong Association helping out the elderly Hmong program. She worked for the minimum wage ($4.25). Because of their family size, they were still eligible for low-income housing assistance. Another man I met worked at a car dealership washing cars for $5.00 an hour. His wife was unable to work because of the small children still at home. They needed the assistance of AFDC to supplement his wages.

Families that were the most successful were those which had combined wage and non-wage incomes. For instance, Tou D's family consisted of himself, his wife and mother, his five children, and a female relative and her three children. He and his wife both worked at factory jobs that paid $6.50 an hour. His mother was elderly and received SSI. His oldest son worked at a local grocery store, and his female relative received AFDC for herself and her three children. She also watched the non-school age children when Tou and his wife worked. All totaled, the family was able to save enough money for a down payment on a duplex apartment after their third year in the United States.

The Hmong Mutual Association serves the Hmong community with information about jobs, training programs, and placement. Employment and educational training programs like the Key States Initiative (KSI) are administered through the Hmong Association. KSI is a federally-funded program designed to place refugees in jobs so as to eliminate or reduce their reliance on welfare (see Fass, 1991). The Hmong Association works closely with local employers in setting up training positions for Southeast Asian Refugees. Programs have also been set up at the local technical college to give refugees the needed training and job skills for various occupations.

One example has been training in the construction and rehabilitation of houses. A Vocational Language Cluster Training program has been set up at various companies who hire refugees; this program gives language assistance to employees for on-the-job training as well as classroom time for language learning. The program's success has contributed to the Hmong community's initiative to help refugees find employment. It also helped with the cooperation and interest of Wausau's business community concerned with reducing the welfare rolls.

Recently, other jobs have opened up for the Hmong. After completing technical training programs or college degrees, Hmong individuals have been recruited into the police force, into the hospital staff as technicians, the funeral home business, and the schools as teachers and counselors.

The Hmong pursue a host of other activities and ventures to make additional income. Information about income-earning opportunities is usually channeled first to those working in refugee services or at the Hmong Mutual Association. These people assess the economic value of the job and then call the appropriate people to fill it. Although workers in refugee services are told to be impartial in dispensing job information within the Hmong community, it is their relatives they first think of when income earning opportunities arise.

Several families in the Madison area, for instance, initially became involved in home production work, assembling electronic parts for a local manufacturer. They learned of the opportunity through a cousin who worked at a local office for refugee services. After the families had proven their reliability, the manufacturing company then made all further contacts directly with the families when additional home work became available.

In one case, the electronic assembling work at home involved all the members of an extended family household, consisting of a husband, his wife and three children and his elderly parents. Though the husband and wife had full-time jobs, they saw the home work as a way to save more money. While they worked during the day, the husband's parents worked on the project. Then during the evening, after dinner, the rest of the family gathered around the table to work. The family was paid on a piece-rate basis. As I watched the sixty-four year-old grandmother trimming the plastic parts with a razor blade, I asked her if the work was hard. She smiled and said: "It's the same as doing the *paj ntaub* needlework, only I get paid more to do this."

The children were aware of their parents' finances and how much was to be gained by doing this home work. The young son (age seven) told me: "If we work fast and do a good job, the company will ask us to help them again." Clearly, the children were being instructed in the value of being hardworking, efficient, and reliable. Other cultural values, that of family cooperation and the interdependence of family members, and of saving and working towards a future goal, were also being taught. Other families stressed these same work-related cultural values and attitudes to their children. Caplan, Whitmore, and Choy found similar core values among the Boat people from Indochina. Ninety-eight percent of the refugees sampled in their study agreed that education and achievement, a cohesive family unit, and hard work were the three most important values for them (1989: 42).

## AGRICULTURAL LABOR AND WOMEN'S WORK

Unlike men who may refuse work that appears to lower their status, Hmong women are more flexible and apt to take jobs that bring money into the household without regard to status. The majority of jobs for women in the Wausau area are seasonal and agricultural.

Ginseng production, or *shang* as most people call it around the Wausau area, provides summer employment for many Hmong women and youth. Ginseng, a root highly valued by Asian cultures for its folk medicinal value, can be found growing in the "wild" from Kentucky to Northern Canada. The ginseng in the Wausau and Marathon County area is cultivated ginseng and accounts for about 95 percent of all ginseng sold in the United States.

In order to duplicate the deep-woods environment of wild ginseng, cultivators have to artificially create shade. The countryside around Wausau is dotted with areas of low-posted structures, covered by a lattice of wooden slates and netting to protect the plants from the sun. Some of the structures are as low as four feet and require the worker to stoop down over the beds to pull weeds and cultivate the plants.

Over 3000 acres of artifically-shaded areas are utilized for growing ginseng in Wisconsin. With an annual production of 1.3 to 1.5 million pounds of harvested root, ginseng is one of Wisconsin's most valuable crops on a per-acre basis, yielding between fifty million to seventy million dollars annually. After it is harvested, most of the ginseng crop is exported to Korea and China.

The production of ginseng has actually increased with the arrival of the Hmong to Marathon County. Prior to the 1980s, the production level was low because of labor shortages. High school students worked the ginseng during the weeding stage in the summer months. However, by the time the ginseng was ready to harvest, the students were back in school. With the influx of Southeast Asian refugees into Marathon County, and their willingness to do intensive farm labor, more land was converted to ginseng gardens. Hmong women were able to provide the labor needed during the ginseng growing season and are now the predominant workers in its production.

Women participate in the ginseng fields as a group rather than as individual laborers. Since ginseng work is sporadic and depends on the weather, it requires close contact with farmers who need laborers at a moment's notice. Women will form work groups made up of relatives and friends, with one person designated as the leader and go-between for them and the farmer. The leader is usually a woman who has fairly adequate English-speaking abilities and available transportation. The leader will then call the ginseng farmers to arrange for work and bring out the team for the days that are needed.

A good leader will try to get the best wages and the most work hours, and guard the team against unfair work conditions. There are some ginseng owners that many team leaders avoid due to low pay and unsafe working conditions. The lack of outdoor toilets, and a disrespectful, attitude (in the form of verbal abuse or accusations of stealing the owner's ginseng roots) have been the cause for some of the complaints that Hmong women have lodged against several ginseng owners.

Wages paid for ginseng work vary from farm to farm, and ranged from $6.00 to $8.00 per hour in 1991. Some farmers pay in cash, whereas others write checks and deduct taxes. Some ginseng owners pay the team leader a lump sum and then let her distribute the money to the workers, according to the fee that she has set in advance with the team. In some cases, the leader may take a certain percentage of the wages as compensation for finding the team work.

Although many Hmong women I talked with looked forward to opportunities to work in the ginseng fields, non-Hmong people complained about the unreliability of the Hmong as workers. One man whose brother owns a ginseng garden complained that his brother can never get enough Hmong rounded up to work. He continued: "They work only when they want to or when they need the money. They might tell you they will come back tomorrow but then they never show up."

One young married woman admitted to me that she was not very regular as a ginseng worker. In her early twenties, she has a regular full-time job during the school year as a bilingual teacher's aide. Her husband also works full-time in a local factory. She told me that she works the ginseng fields mainly for something to do and that she enjoys the extra cash. But she said that the work is hard on the back, from having to stoop all day long under the lattice structures. After three straight days of this kind of work, she usually takes a break.

Teams can fall apart easily if one member cancels due to an illness or emergency in the family. If team members are not proficient in English, making an appointment with a doctor can be difficult, time consuming, and require the aid of many people. Help is needed in making the phone call, in transportation and interpreting, and in childcare while the team member is at the doctor's office.

Transportation is another problem. Many women go to the fields in one vehicle. If the team's driver is unable to work one day, this means the rest of the team has no way to get to the ginseng fields. If none of the other women has a driver's license or access to a vehicle, then none of the team can show up for work.

Also ginseng work is sporadic. Workers can find themselves working for three to four days straight, putting in long hours, and then going for several weeks with no work at all. In the meantime, women might take on additional seasonal jobs, working on other agricultural crops such as cucumber, corn and tobacco fields. Many times the demands of these crops overlap with the ginseng workload, creating the appearance to the ginseng owners that the Hmong are not interested in working, when in fact they are working various jobs already.

Labor for the ginseng gardens also attracts workers outside of the local population. Hmong families often call relatives in other areas of Wisconsin and from nearby states to come during the peak work seasons. These relatives may stay for the weekend or several weeks, depending on their commitments at home, and work as part of a team in the ginseng harvest. I knew several families whose relatives came from Oshkosh and St. Paul to help with the ginseng, thus combining visiting with the opportunity to make some extra money. Having relatives come to visit created a celebratory atmosphere in the households and fields. One woman described the time when her relatives came for several weeks from St. Paul to work in the ginseng gardens:

> It was a happy time for everyone. Everyone goes out there, and as we work we start to tell stories. One lady might start by telling about her life in Laos and then the next thing you know everyone is talking. It reminds me of the sound of popcorn cooking. That's what it's like. Everybody just popping, telling stories, laughing.

Women of the Hmong Christian Missionary Alliance Church also get involved in the ginseng gardens as a work group. During one Sunday's service, a leader from the women's group announced that they needed volunteers to work the ginseng. They were trying to get a team of workers together who would be willing to donate a day's worth of wages in the gardens as part of a church fund-raising project.

Hmong women also form teams to work the corn fields for canning companies. Many Hmong women I knew in the Madison area were hired by Libby Foods to weed and detassel the corn in the fields. Transportation was usually provided to the team of workers, taking them to the work sites and then returning them home.

One female team leader in Madison was able to get together women from her church to work. The team was so successful the first year in the corn field that she paid the airfare to bring relatives from California to work on her team the next summer. During this second summer, the team leader boasted that her team, which consisted of twenty relatives, made $40,000 in the two week period. One relative suggested they pool these resources each summer to help each family buy a house.

The money seems phenomenal when viewed as a lump sum, as the Hmong view it. But to earn this money, they usually worked fifteen hour days in the hot sun. Rarely, though, did I hear complaints about the work or the working conditions. Most families saw the work as enjoyable and as giving them something to do. The leader who brought her relatives from California to work for the two weeks commented: "We all go work in the fields just like back home [in Laos]. We work together, help each other, laugh, and just have a lot of fun, and earn money too!"

## Cash Cropping

From tiny herbal gardens in their yards to vegetable plots found throughout the city and countryside, Hmong involvement in agricultural practices extends in the summer growing season to include cash-cropping. In the Wisconsin area, the common cash crop is cucumbers. People belonging to the same sub-lineage will rent an acre or two of land from a farmer who will till the land and provide the seeds. The women then plant and tend the fields, weeding, hoeing, and watering from around May to August.

Work in the cucumber fields during harvest time is labor intensive and requires the whole family's cooperation while the women put in long hours in the fields. I have observed women leaving their house as early as 4:00 A.M. and not returning until 8:00 P.M. or later. Food and water are packed for the day in ice chests and often prepared the night before. While the women are working in the fields, household and childcare duties fall to either the wife's husband, his or her elderly parents or relatives, or to older children. In nuclear family households with young children and a husband working a full-time job, the children are usually taken to a relative's house for the two to three weeks duration of the August harvest.

During the harvest, some cucumbers are kept back for personal consumption, eaten raw or boiled. The majority, however, are sold back to the farmer who rents them the land. The price of the crop is based on the size of the cucumbers which are ranked from the smallest (size 1) to the largest (size 6). Rates in 1991 ranged from $24.00 per one hundred pounds for size one down to $3.00 per one hundred pounds for size six.

It was difficult to get anyone to tell me exactly how much they made in a cucumber field in a summer. I would get answers such as "not much," "only a little," or "maybe two hundred dollars." Most Hmong people I met had no reservations about telling me their rent or mortgage payments, their wages or how much they paid for something. They were reluctant to answer my questions on cucumber earnings because many families involved in cucumber farming were on welfare and may not have been reporting what they made from growing cucumbers.

One man finally told me that a family can make around one to two-thousand dollars an acre, depending on the weather. The income must be reported to AFDC, he said. When telling me this, he became emotional:

The Hmong people want to work, and they work very hard in the fields and report their money to AFDC only to get their checks cut. It hardly seems fair because they don't earn that much out there. But AFDC cuts their check and it is hard because the families have already planned and budgeted their AFDC check amount to pay for the car, food, and gas. They are working but it doesn't seem to get them ahead when the checks get cut. Many Hmong people feel they are just working for Bill [the owner of the land]. And Bill makes a lot of money selling the pickles at a higher price to the factories.

I knew families who came up from Madison to spend the whole summer with relatives in Steven's Point and Wausau solely to work in the cucumber fields. One family in Steven's Point even moved several small trailers out to the land and turned the work situation into a summer vacation for the children. Other families followed suit, some building temporary shacks at the edge of the land which caused anger because the local community considered them to be "unsightly" structures.

The Hmong believe that they should be able to work hard and still get the same amount of AFDC. When their welfare checks are cut because they report earned income, they become discouraged and look for ways to get around the regulations. Households try to be flexible. Subsistence activities increase the amount of available cash from welfare payments that can be used for non-food goods. Household members who do not have earned income from a job have the time to pursue subsistence activities, thus diversifying the types of income coming into the household. Cucumber farming is seen by many Hmong families as an extension of gardening and other subsistence activities (see Chapter 6). When a household has several members working full-time in the labor market, unemployed members (especially women) can still remain active participants in the economic success of the household by pursuing various kinds of subsistence activities.

## ETHNIC BUSINESSES AND ENTERPRISES

A host of ethnic businesses and enterprises have sprung up within the Hmong communities in Wisconsin. Wausau has four ethnic food stores which are owned and operated by Hmong families. In addition there is now a Hmong-owned meat market, two restaurants that specialize in Lao food and cater to the general public, two video stores, a video games-arcade, and a small shoe company.

Individual and self-employment activities were also evident in the community. Many Hmong women in the Wausau area are actively involved in selling Amway, Avon, and Mary Kay products. One Hmong man from Wausau sold Kirby vacuum sweepers throughout the Midwest, marketing his sweepers to relatives and clanspeople living in Wisconsin, Minnesota, Michigan, Illinois, and as far south as Kansas City, Missouri. Several families also sold garden produce as well as their *paj ntaub* needlework pieces at the local farmers' market.

Most of the people who were involved in these sorts of marketing activities had been living in the United States between seven to ten years or longer, and had a good to excellent command of English. They also had jobs in which they developed some friendships outside of the Hmong community. Most were also actively involved in the Hmong Christian and Missianary Alliance church (HCMA). In most cases, their customers were drawn from the Hmong community, either through church groups or through extended kinship networking.

## WOMEN AND ETHNIC ENTERPRISES

Hmong who were not very proficient in the English language were still able to participate in income-producing activities by targeting their products or services towards the "traditional" needs in the community.

Traditionally, Hmong had no role as traders. The Hmong household and village was basically a self-sufficient unit. Households grew enough rice and corn to last at least fifteen months (S. Yang 1980: 12) and raised pigs, chickens, and other livestock. Needs could be fulfilled by trading items along family lines (Lemoine, 1972: 158–9).

Prior to 1940, Hmong villages in Laos would be visited by traders, usually Chinese, during the dry season. Arriving on pack animals, these traders supplied the Hmong with iron, metal pots and pans, flints, matches, sulfur for making gunpowder, salt, thread, cloth, and other wares. Payment for goods was in the form of barter, usually raw opium, but also in the form of crops, baskets, and silver (Bernatzik, 1947/1970: 568–69).

For many Hmong, traditional farming life had been severely disrupted during the period from 1955 until U.S. troops were pulled out of Vietnam in 1975. As Hmong men joined the escalating military operations, Hmong villages were deprived of male labor for the planting seasons. Villages became dependent on air drops of rice and other staples during this time. In the 1960s, a market economy in refugee resettlement towns, bolstered by military payrolls, engaged more and more Hmong in supplementing their agricultural lifestyle through both buying and selling as well as wage work. (Barney, 1967: 289–90).

Despite a disruption of their traditional way of life, their uprooting and relocation into large population centers created a number of economic circumstances, of which the Hmong were quick to take advantage. Wages paid to Hmong soldiers enabled many families to start up a small business or engage in some sort of trade; these wages supplemented and, in many cases, replaced their life as self-sufficient farmers. Traders, middlemen, and brokers appeared, and more and more shops opened, selling fabrics, shoes, clothes, noodles, meats and vegetables. Larger businesses, industries and professions also opened up for the Hmong. Quincy writes:

> Some enterprising Hmong built an ice factory at Long Cheng, while others opened restaurants. Hmong also took up new professions. There were Hmong photographers and Hmong dentists; Hmong became tailors, bakers, cobblers and radio repairmen. The new cottage industry, the fabrication of brooms, blossomed in the outlying villages giving employment to over 200 Hmong families (1988: 183).

One of the most profitable enterprises for the Hmong was the taxi business. Over 80 percent of the taxis in operation in Laos during the Vietnam War were owned by Hmong. By combining their resources, Hmong families bought jeeps through military channels to provide taxi services along the dirt roads connecting the three major relocation towns of Sam Thong, Long Cheng, and Muong Cha (Yang, 1980: 12).

Although information about business enterprises during the war period is slim, they may very well have set the stage for Hmong women's trading of goods in the United States. Wartime provided opportunities for Hmong women to step out of their traditional roles. Nancy Donnelly's life history interview with

May Xiong shows how she was able to use her husband's soldier wages to increase their income. She traded chickens, fabric and household goods between her village, Long Tieng, and the front (Xiong and Donnelly, 1986: 222–23).

In Wausau and Madison I observed Hmong women acting as traders and peddlers (called *ko taw muag*) in their communities. Women sold and bartered a variety of goods from traditional needlework, embroidery thread, cloth, herbs and medicines to jewelry, French silver coins, and clothing.

Hmong women sent money to their relatives and their husband's relatives in the Thailand refugee camps. In return, the women requested that relatives send items that they knew were marketable in the United States, the *paj ntaub* story cloths being perhaps the most popular. The story cloths, however, usually only get marketed to the non-Hmong population, with about half of the proceeds from sales going back to Thailand to support relatives in the refugee camps. The marketing of the story cloths to non-Hmong consumers has been examined by Donnelly (1986, 1994) and Erik Cohen (1989). Donnelly concludes that, even though the marketing is done by the women, the needlework pieces and the cash from their sales move along patrilineal kinship networks (1994: 111–12).

Other needlework items sent over from the camps are marketed solely to the Hmong community. Such items include all the pieces of a woman's New Year's outfit—skirts, jackets, beaded aprons, hats, coin purses, silver necklaces, and earrings. Supplies from the homeland also include items necessary for daily Hmong life, including baby carriers, baby hats, funeral items, lucky charm necklaces, and herbs. Although many of these items are obtained through patrilineal kinship networks, they are marketed in the United States to both relatives and non-relatives.

When I first asked about Hmong needlework sales in the Wausau area, I was told by non-Hmong social service workers that sales were not successful and that many women in the area were not interested in needlework. I was surprised when I found a lively market for stitchery within the Hmong community. Almost every woman I met had needlework items that she would sell. These items were either made by her or received from relatives in the camps.

When I asked Hmong women why they did not sell their needlework at public locations which were trying to promote Hmong needlework sales, such as Lutheran Social Services or the Neighbor's Place, they remarked that Americans were not interested in buying these items or had no use for them. Hmong women had the most success selling needlework during summer craft fairs held around the Midwest. Even then, the most popular items sold were wall hangings or decorative pieces for the U.S. home rather than items that were traditionally useful to the Hmong.

Once a package from the homeland arrives at the woman's home, she is usually out that very day marketing it to relatives and interested friends. I observed women initiating contacts first by phone and then either walking or driving over to various relatives' houses to peddle the items. For instance, a woman named Xai received embroidery thread from her father who was still in the Thailand camps. She sorted the threads out by color and then bundled up a variety of them to sell during her ESL class that afternoon. During the evening she went to participate in the Hmong church choir, again taking the threads with her to hawk during breaks.

Another woman, Tong, received six baby carriers in the morning mail and sold all six that afternoon at her ESL class. Before class started she pulled the baby carriers out to show a few women. Before I knew it, all the Hmong women in the class gathered

Hmong women trading embroidery thread during a break in their ESL class.

tightly around her, examining the stitching and asking the price. She was selling them for $25.00 each. Xai, the woman who had sold the embroidery thread just days before, bargained with Tong to get a lower price for two of the carriers. Xai was buying the baby carriers as gifts for her two nieces living in St. Paul.

The baby carriers were sold without collecting any money. Tong just told everyone to pay her when they could. Nothing was written down. The women took their baby carriers home after class and paid Tong in cash during the next class session.

Another case worth noting is the woman who received a package containing lucky charms from Laos. The woman went to one of the Hmong food stores in Wausau and announced her wares to the owner. Immediately word spread throughout the community of the shipment. A Hmong woman I knew was interested in purchasing a pair of charms. She was on the phone with the seller for over half an hour trying to negotiate a price. When she got off the phone she explained the value of these charms to me:

> These are very rare charms made in Laos and they are very valuable. You need to buy two to make a complete set and for them to work properly. She has two that I really want. One is in the shape of a gourd. This is very good fortune. We have a story about the king who put all his riches in a gourd so that no one would take his daughter away from him. The second charm is a rhinoceros. This is a very lucky animal and very powerful. Medicine is made from its horn and it is also a very ancient symbol in Chinese culture. Both charms together would be very powerful for the owner. I tried to get this woman to sell them a little cheaper but she refused. She wants $225 for each or two for $400. Actually that is still a very good price because they are made of silver and are very heavy. Only the very old timers and the rich Hmong own them. I really want some too, but I must talk with my husband about it.

Besides selling the charms, the woman also received silver necklaces and bracelets from Laos which she was selling for $20.00 to $30.00 each.

Within the ethnic community, sales from needlework and other items were thus brisk and reflected a market which catered to the Hmong rather than non-Hmong consumer. Clearly, Hmong consumers are making spending decisions which go beyond their basic day-to-day needs and are buying products which increase their sense of identity as Hmong. The items purchased are exactly those which allow them to display their Hmongness within their community. Furthermore, families able to afford the symbolic representations of Hmongness, such as clothing and jewelry, gain status and recognition within their communities for their economic success as Hmong in America. Their success as Hmong in America is linked with their success at being "American" (which to them implies wealth), while maintaining at the same time, their separateness as Hmong. Thus, some of the items they purchase are not only expensive, but also symbolic.

Packages from the homeland therefore become more than personal gifts or supplemental income for an individual family. As homeland goods and Hmong-made goods are marketed, they carry with them the potential to bring symbolic wealth to the whole community. People purchase items that help them maintain a lifestyle, food preferences, traditions, religious and spiritual beliefs, and ultimately their identities as Hmong in the United States.

## Selling "Asian" Clothing

Traditionally, Hmong identities have been based in part on the type of clothing worn and the embroidery work that decorates it. Women's dresses with embroidery designs carry the markers of identity for individual clans, subgroups, and regions. Blue Hmong women traditionally wore indigo-colored pleated skirts with embroidery designs. The White Hmong women traditionally wore two different outfits. A white pleated skirt without any adornment was reserved for special occasions, and loose black pants and shirt were worn every day. In the United States, the traditional dress has been dropped from everyday wear and is usually worn only on special occasions such as New Year celebrations. Due to a conscious need to fit in and be less conspicuous in U.S. society, women prefer to wear Western-looking clothes.

Despite the absence of traditional dress, many women continue to dress in ways that signal to one another that they are still Hmong. Older women and young married women who have recently arrived in the United States prefer wearing below-the-knee polyester skirts with printed designs. Button-up sweaters have also recently been a popular addition to the Hmong wardrobe in the United States. Many "Asian" clothes, as they call them, are bought from the local ethnic food stores or from women peddlers in the neighborhood. Skirts and sweaters are purchased from California wholesale houses in which other Asian groups manufacture and market clothing specifically tarketed to "Asian" people. As a woman named Zer told me, the clothes fit because they are made for smaller body sizes. Talking in general about shopping for clothes in the United States, Zer commented: "Everything is too big in America. We need 'Asian' clothes. We can't buy pants because the legs are too long for our men, and the ties are too long and too wide."

One family in Madison was involved with marketing acrylic "Asian" sweaters. Chia was able to purchase the sweaters at cost from her mother who owned an ethnic food store in Southern California and bought the sweaters wholesale from an Asian clothing factory. The sweaters were sent to Chia in bundles of fifty or more in various sizes and colors. Chia and her mother-in-law then peddled the sweaters to the women in the Madison area.

Starting first in their own neighborhood, the two women went door to door to Hmong homes to "pay a visit" to each woman and show the sweaters. Once in the home, other women began arriving to see the sweaters, sometimes being called over by phone or sent for by one of the children. Trying on the sweaters, especially in the presence of a group, created a festive and entertaining atmosphere for buying. The sweaters sold for $25.00 to $35.00, and discounts given if one bought two or more.

Although direct pressure techniques were not used, a good many suggestions were made as to why a Hmong woman ought to have one of the sweaters. They were attractive, warm, washable, and long lasting. It was even suggested at several houses that they would make good gifts for Mother's Day, which at the time, was soon approaching.

Chia and her mother-in-law took the sweaters with them to sell during women's church gatherings, prayer meetings, and on visits to relatives in other cities. The sweaters were hardly ever paid for at the time they were taken. As in the case of the baby carriers, Hmong consumers paid when they were able. Written records were never kept of who purchased and who paid for the sweaters. It was all based on an honor system and, most likely, the memory necessary in an oral-based culture.

The sweater-selling enterprise lasted for about six months, until the women exhausted all their available channels for selling the sweaters. Shortly afterwards, Chia received a bundle of men's ties from her mother to sell for $8.00 each.

In both cases, the women initially marketed the sweaters and ties within their kinship network and gradually expanded out to all Hmong women in the area, then within the state, and then across state lines. Although I had expected to find that the principal channels of cooperation and transaction would lie within patrilineal connections (see Donnelly, 1994: 111–112), I was surprised that women were utilizing both affinal and consanguineal relations. This allowed the women to open as many channels as possible for business ventures, regardless of affinal clan ties.

There were other clothing enterprises, too. While visiting in St. Paul for the week, several unmarried women from the Yang clan bought men's pullover shirts at a discount store and decorated them with strips of Hmong needlework designs. They then marketed them to Hmong college students as ethnic clothing. The shirts sold for $25.00 to $35.00. Similar clothing ideas were also marketed at the yearly St. Paul soccer games, in which Hmong individuals rented booth space to sell everything from clothes to video tapes, cassette recordings, traditional clothing, herbs, posters, and food.

Most of the ethnic enterprises I have mentioned remain small scale, temporary, and operate out of the home. The amount of capital necessary to get started was small, and individuals seemed excited about their ventures. There was a flexibility in marketing new products and in trying to create needs and wants in the Hmong consumer market. There was a continual testing of the market and the challenge of trying to offer a product that no one else had. Most individuals viewed these enterprises as a way to make some extra cash; they did not see them as something they wanted to do on a permanent basis or on a larger scale.

## CONCLUSION

Some of the economic activities I have described are lodged within an informal economy. These activities take on the quality of "Hmong" work, work which many Hmong feel they can do well because they have the know-how from their historical past. Ethnic enterprises, while capitalizing mainly on the ethnic community, reinforce a sense of Hmongness.

Hmong ethnic-based shops and stores and ethnic goods and services provide a tangible link to "Old World" tastes and cultural traditions, and refashion the "New World" in a design familiar to the homeland. Yet Hmong ethnic activities are not provincial. They do not reflect a preference for the comforts of "Old World" routines and a longing for the past.

Hmong entreprenurial experiences during the war years suggests that, although many come to the United States lacking a cultural background or experience with Western ways, they do not lack experience with capitalism. Their experiences with cash cropping and trading and small business enterprises during relocation and while in refugee camps may very well have set the tone for their adaptive strategies in the United States.

Hmong enterprises in the United States exploit their knowledge of homeland routines in order to capitalize on the present. Far from maintaining the familiar world of homeland, Hmong ethnic enterprises and work create new channels of opportunities and ways of exploring the economic environment of the United States.

The most exciting aspect of Hmong entreprenurial activities is how easily they fit into the social structure and networks of the group. The channels of activity are flexible, creative, kin-oriented, and adapted to the Hmong diaspora. Their enterprises and entreprenurial schemes are experimental in nature. One gets the feeling that the Hmong are trying out various entreprenurial activities while exploring the possibilities of how to make money in the United States. Goods and services do not just fill "Old World" wants and needs, but create new desires for goods which carry symbolic statements of identity and what it means to be Hmong in the United States.

## NOTES

1. The Hmong Resettlement Studies were carried out in Portland, Oregon (Sweeney, et al., 1984); Fresno, California (Reder, et al., 1983); Orange County, California (Cohn, et al., 1984); Minneapolis-St. Paul, Minnesota (Downing, 1984c); Providence, Rhode Island (Finck, 1984); Dallas-Fort Worth, Texas (Downing, 1984a); and Fort Smith, Arkansas (Downing, 1984b).

# 6

# Hmong Views on Self-Sufficiency

**Z**uag, a seventy-nine-year-old woman, was standing barefoot in her tiny garden when I arrived at her house early in June. Zuag pointed out the different vegetables she was growing as she stooped and hoed the earth. She had planted onions, mustard greens, peas and carrots, and some various herbs. This was her garden. Her son plowed the twelve by twelve foot plot of ground in the backyard of their duplex home so that she had something to do and would not be lonely. Her two daughters-in-law had much bigger gardens on the outskirts of Wausau. It was their gardens that provided the stock of vegetable foods that would last the family throughout the winter. Zuag's garden, nevertheless, provided her with the satisfaction of growing food for immediate use in the kitchen.

Bronislaw Malinowski said of the Trobrianders of Papua New Guinea that if you want to know who they are as a people, go to their gardens (1935: xix). A similar statement could be made about the Hmong. From their gardens we can learn about Hmong food, and how it is grown, processed, eaten, and preserved. We also can learn about their ideas of nutrition and health, eating habits, ritual behavior, and family attitudes and values. Most importantly, gardens are an economic asset to Hmong families. And as an asset, gardens reflect Hmong attitudes and values toward family, work, saving, spending, and sharing. To understand the value and importance of gardens for Hmong families is to gain insight into their views of self-sufficiency and independence.

## Ethnographic Background

Before the disruption of war, the vast majority of Hmong in Laos grew crops in swidden. Their agricultural and subsistence cycle consisted of burning off the fields and preparing them for planting. They grew rice, corn, a variety of vegetable crops, and maintained a cash crop of opium (Bernatzik, 1947/1970: 385–86; Tapp, 1989: 470). The Hmong also gathered wild roots, tubers, fruits, and other vegetables and herbs to supplement their diets. They practiced animal husbandry, raising pigs, goats, chickens, some cattle, buffalo, and horses. The men engaged in hunting and fishing activities as a further means of subsistence (Copper, et al., 1991).

At the same time, women weaved cloth, sewed, and embroidered their clothes. The men did metal-smithing, basketry, jewelry, and carpentry. They also made many of their own tools. The cash obtained from the sale of opium was used to purchase items that they could not grow or make themselves. All in all, most Hmong were relatively self-sufficient and independent from the larger market economies.

When Hmong people talk about their homeland in comparison to the United States, many describe a peaceful life in the mountains free from bills or debts. Although life was hard because of the strenuous daily physical labor of farming, most Hmong told me, "We owned our own land. We had no bills. We provided for ourselves." Talk about life in the United States almost always includes mention of one main complaint: there are too many bills to pay. It is the bills that make them say the United States is not the land of freedom.

This attitude of wanting to be self-sufficient and independent of a larger system carries over into Hmong life in the United States. A prominent Hmong spokesman in the Madison area told me that the Hmong look for all sorts of ways to "escape" the bills and expenses that are a part of U.S. lifestyle. They will do whatever it takes to lower their cost of living expenses. He stated: "This means growing all their own food so that they don't have to buy it, hunt and fish, everything. They look for ways that will not cost them much to eat."

In addition to hunting, gathering, fishing, and gardening, Hmong families take full advantage of available social and financial resources as well. Entitlement programs such as SSI, and AFDC; low-income housing, food stamps, medical assistance, fuel assistance, the Women, Infants, and Children (WIC) program for pregnant and nursing mothers; and government and charity give-away programs for free food, clothing, and furniture are all seen as resources that can cut down on bills. Furthermore, Hmong families purchase items at yard sales, Goodwill stores, and wholesale houses to lower the cost of living expenses. One Hmong woman, working in the United States for over ten years, explained her perception of the social welfare system to me:

> The benefits and money for these programs have been there for one hundred years. They are for the people who want to use them or apply for them. They [Americans] must not want the money because they don't try to find out about it. If it's there, why not use it. If they don't want it, that's their problem.

## GARDENING PRACTICES AND SELF-SUFFICIENCY

Almost every Hmong family that I met had a vegetable garden. Even the tiniest spaces, like the areas typically used for flower gardens, were planted with a variety of herbs and vegetables for daily use. Most families, however, have plots larger than flower gardens.

Hmong families in the Madison area have access to land through the Community Action Commission (CAC) Garden Program. Gardeners are able to get additional plots on a first-come basis. Sometimes Hmong families manage to get three or more plots for themselves.

Gardening activities in Wausau have a much different flavor. Women's garden plots are larger and they are scattered and isolated from other women's gardens, rather than clustered in a communal setting like Madison. There are, however, several communal garden areas in Wausau. One was behind a low-income housing project which provided garden space for the families. Another was just outside of the city near the Hmong Church. Other than these, most Hmong families make arrangements with local farmers in the Wausau area to gain access to land. Some families pay a fee for land use while others get plots free based on friendships formed with farmers as employees or summer laborers in the ginseng fields.

During the month of February I watched families prepare for the planting season by starting pepper and tomato plants from seed. Furniture was moved and rearranged to make room for the seedlings to be placed on tables and sills in every available sunny window.

Seeds for the spring's planting are stored in buckets and jars or are wrapped in pieces of newspaper or plastic. These were their seeds from last year's harvest, collected and dried in the sun for this year's garden. Hmong women hardly ever buy expensive pre-packaged seeds. Some seeds were initially sent over by relatives in Thailand as starter seeds for the vegetables they missed and were unable to buy in the United States. Seeds become treasured gift and trade items among women who have not yet acquired a stock of seeds for a yearly garden. But seeds are mainly given freely to others, usually with concern that now they too can have a successful garden and be able to feed their family well.

I have always been a gardener myself, but I became more deeply connected to the Hmong through my initial gardening experiences when I lived in Madison. Ying J., a woman in her late fifties, took it upon herself to initiate me into the art of Hmong gardening. "We will plant the fields" (*Peb yuav cog ua teb*"), she said to me excitedly the night that she and her daughter-in-law Chia A. took me out to our garden plots behind the Madison Coliseum. These are the words Hmong people use, she said, when they go to the fields. Her voice was full of excitement as she grabbed her Hmong hoe and long handled knife and headed up the hillside just beyond the gardens. On the hilltop was a thicket of trees. Ying gathered up the dried sticks and piled them into bundles and then called to her daughter-in-law to help her. The sticks would be used in the garden as support poles, eventually forming lattice-like fences for the peas and long beans to climb on. I later came to recognize the differences between Hmong and non-Hmong gardens in Wausau as I located these same structures dotting the countryside. Ying smiled as she tossed her bundle down onto the others. As she did so she said: "In Laos I could farm this whole area of land by myself," waving her hand across the landscape. "These little pieces [the plots] are nothing to what I am used to doing."

Gardens are usually spoken of as *niam teb*, mother's land, for it is the women who do the planting, weeding, watering, and harvesting. Their husbands may come out initially to see the site, help break up the soil if necessary, and occasionally water the plants. But in the gardens, a husband is under the supervision of his wife. She is the one responsible for the success of the garden, and the one who decides what to plant, where to plant, and how much to plant.

The gardens are busiest during the early morning hours and again in the evenings until dark. Older women are usually in the gardens in the morning while their daughters-in-law come in the evenings, after the children are home from school.

In the evenings at the communal gardens there are always a lot of children. They are brought out to the gardens to play. Even the families with non-communal gardens are never alone there. The family or several female relatives and their children will go to their plot of land before dinner-time to work and play. Girls around seven years or older usually help their mother by carrying buckets of water to the plants or by watching younger children while their mother does the hoeing and weeding. Sometimes a mother will strap the youngest child into a baby carrier on her back while she hoes, or she will strap the baby onto one of her older daughter's back. Occasionally a mother may look up to check on her children and then wander over to another woman's plot, taking the time to examine the plants, chit-chat, and catch up on gossip.

Hmong women take full advantage of the growing season by planting a variety of crops with short and long maturation cycles. The faster growing plants like mustard greens, onion sets, and peas are planted several times in the growing season to provide a continuous harvest of fresh vegetables while waiting for the slower growth plants like tomatoes, cabbage, pumpkins and squash to ripen.

Hmong women use many of the plants before they are ripe to prepare meals. One woman told me:

> We Hmong do not just eat the vegetables like Americans. We also eat the plant. Like the squash; we eat the leaves and stems too. Just boil them with the meat. The sugar peas—we do the same. We pick off the end stems and cook them like greens. It does not harm the plant; they grow more. If you want the peas, then you don't pick the leaves.

Gardening connects Hmong women to their past, their traditional chores in Laos, and provides a sense of worth for them now

Hmong woman returning home from planting
her garden in Wausau.

that they are in the United States. Unlike their husbands, many of
whom have lost their traditional roles as agriculturalists who
cleared the land, built their own houses and made their own
tools, the women continue the traditional duties of cooking, sewing, raising their children and gardening.

I rarely met a married woman who did not have a vegetable
plot. Women who were employed full-time made every effort to
find time to garden. At times, however, it proved to be a hapless
endeavor for women with full-time jobs.

Mai C., a woman in Wausau who was in her early thirties and
under extreme pressure in her job as an interpreter and cultural
broker for the Hmong community, still found time three nights a
week to go to her garden. Mai's day usually begins at 6 A.M. when
she gets her two preschool-aged children dressed and ready to go
to their aunt's house for the day. Between this time and 7:30,
when she leaves for work, her phone will have rung at least a half
a dozen times. Relatives call asking favors or wanting her to come
by to translate a letter. Others call asking her to come to the hospi-

tal to interpret or explain a medical procedure to a family member refusing surgery. The requests are always urgent and seemingly at the crisis state when Mai is called. While weeding her garden one evening she told me:

> People depend on me, I must help them. They are my people. There is so much they don't understand about American culture. But I am getting burned out. It is just too easy for people to call me without trying to solve their problems by themselves. That is why I like it out here [in my garden]. You know, when I was younger I didn't really much like to have a garden. But now that I am getting older I like it a lot. I like the fact that I can come out here where it is so peaceful and quiet and just work—do something without having to use my brain all the time. It's very relaxing. I can come here and just forget about it all until tomorrow. I grew up on a farm in Laos. My father was a rice farmer. I miss the farm. I miss working on it, being outdoors working. I miss going for water and wood. That's why I like to come out here.

For Mai, gardening provided a respite, a time out of time, in which she could allow herself a sense of detachment from the world of work in which she was in constant demand for her bilingual and bi-cultural knowledge and skills.

Although gardening provides for a continuation of traditional roles, it is given new meaning in the United States. As a tangible link to the past, a woman's gardening activities become imbued with a heightened sense of the past, of past lives and past identities. The act of gardening and the garden sites themselves provide a space for reflexivity in which memories of the home country are arranged and refitted into new patterns of life in the United States.

However, gardening is more than just memories acted out in a new land. It is seen as serious business for every Hmong woman with whom I talked. The fruits of their labor add to and supplement the monetary resources of the family. Hmong gardens are, in many ways, like bank accounts. Hmong identity is marked by the labor women invest in their gardens—and there is the added payoff of saving money.

Chia always enjoyed telling me how the gardens cut down on family food bills. One day, Chia, a bilingual aid for the Madison school district, was having lunch with her non-Hmong co-workers. On that particular day the women were discussing how expensive it was to feed a family. They turned to Chia and said: "You must really have it hard with eight people in your house." Chia said shyly, "not really." As she told me:

> They did not want to believe me when I said that we hardly spend any money on groceries. They wanted to know what we eat, and they thought surely I pay over one-thousand dollars a month for groceries. I just told them,'No I don't'. I tried to explain to them that we grow all our own food and put it in the freezer. But I don't think they believed me. I did not tell them that we buy the meat wholesale, or that we buy a whole cow and split it up with our relatives. I didn't tell them about the fish we catch or the other vegetables we find in the woods. I didn't want them to laugh at me.

Chia is not atypical. Families in Wausau took pride in showing me the food they had stored in their freezers or the vegetables they had preserved. Mee, a woman in her fifties, led me to her back room one day during a visit to her house to show me a room full of squash, pumpkins and other gourds that she would use to feed her family over the winter.

Not being able to talk to non-Hmong about their activities to save money was a topic that came up over and over again, especially in the realm of foraging for food. In addition to gardening, Hmong families in Wausau and Madison gather mushrooms, nuts and berries, wild apples, various kinds of edible flowers, fiddlesticks, watercress, and a variety of greens and herbs. The gathering of wild edibles takes place in the countryside or along highway and road systems. Hmong also gather edible fruits and vegetables within their local neighborhoods, at parks, and other public places. The location of wild greens and herbs may be spotted while men are out hunting or simply found when a family goes out to their garden or on a picnic at the local park. In households which foraged extensively, even the youngest children were able to identify various edible plants.

In many ways, foraging places are seen as natural extensions of the garden and a resource to be tapped. Hmong attitudes about gathering edible foodstuffs are also shaped by the values they perceive that others in the United States hold. Hmong are well aware that most people in the United States do not engage in foraging activities for subsistence purposes. They find this baffling. Hmong women often express concern over why more "Americans" do not take advantage of these foods that are there just for the taking.

Yet Hmong are also hesitant in talking about their foraging activities. Chia did not tell her American co-workers about her foraging because she was afraid they would laugh at her. Unsure even of my attitude about foraging, she asked me "Do you think it is strange if I told you my people go into the woods and pick food?" When I told her that my grandmother and mother used to do the same, and that my uncle in Oklahoma still forages, she invited me to come with the family the next day to collect watercress (*zaub dej*).

I tagged along on their foraging trip about an hour north of Madison. Six of us each filled a large black plastic garbage bag full of watercress. The family was excited and chattered about the homeland as we sloshed through the swampy creek, bending and cutting the watercress, and slapping off mosquitoes and bugs. Chia's mother-in-law, Ying, remarked:

> This is exactly how it is in Laos. This would be a typical day for us in our country. We would all go out in the fields together to work, or gather the plants, the firewood, the water, and carry them home. We would just go and pick things as we need it. Never have to pay. This way we can save every penny we earn and buy other things with it.

When we had gathered enough watercress Ying called out for us to quit and save some for the others. Other relatives residing in the Madison area as well as a few hours driving distance from the watercress spot would be told of its location.

On our return trip to Madison, Chia again wanted to be assured that I did not think badly of her family for going out and collecting the watercress:

> We do not usually share this information about what we eat with people. It is too personal. Doctors and other people who do not know about our culture have no idea what we eat. We don't tell the doctor everything because it is too difficult to explain it to them. And if we tell them that we go and collect this food they may think that it is

no good for us or that it is poisonous. So we don't tell them these things.

This issue of secrecy came up as well in Wausau, not only concerning foraging but also the preparation and eating of various foods.

Upon returning home, Chia and her mother-in-law divided the watercress into smaller bags and sent the children to deliver the bags to various elderly aunts and uncles. One bag went to Chia's husband's father's oldest brother, one to his father's middle brother, and one to her husband's cousin. Several neighbors who dropped by were each given a small bag. The rest of the watercress was washed and prepared for freezing and pickling.

During the week I spent with the J family in St. Paul, Minnesota, Mrs. J visited the grocery store only once to buy milk and cereal for the children and fruits for snacks. Mrs. J went to her garden daily to pick vegetables for each meal. She also visited the local park twice that week to pick edible flowering plants. She told me she frequents all the local parks for vegetables because they are a tasty treat for her family. She had to be careful about picking the plants in the park, however, because a couple of American women once scolded her for picking the park flowers. She was confused when they told her: "They are to look at, not to eat." She knew she couldn't tell them that they were good to eat too. She laughs now about this episode, saying that she feels she has to "sneak around" when she picks the plants in the park. But she says she will continue because the plants should not go to waste. As for the meat the family used, it had been frozen from hunting and fishing trips or purchased wholesale with Mr. J's two brothers.

## FISHING AND HUNTING

Hunting and fishing represent yet another example of how the Hmong are practicing traditional subsistence activity in the United States in order to save money. Unlike foraging, hunting and fishing do not carry a self-conscious recognition of ethnic difference. Although Hmong recognize that the Americans who engage in hunting activities do so more for sport than subsistence, hunting and fishing are not shrouded in secrecy like foraging activities.

A favorite pastime in the summer months is fishing. Non-working males and older men go fishing, usually taking their grandsons with them. The men go out early in the morning, sometimes bringing home large buckets full of fish, some for the morning breakfast and enough to freeze or pickle. Fishing in the evening and on weekends sometimes includes the whole family. The children are taken to local parks to play while their father fishes, or the family drives to favorite Hmong fishing areas where the men and women chat with other Hmong families while fishing. Teenage boys also take up fishing as a way to get out of the house and be with their friends. One teenage boy I met went fishing everyday after school. He said he enjoyed being outdoors and liked bringing home a big bucket of fish for his mother. He felt it was his way of contributing to the maintenance of the household.

Although many Hmong families I met enjoyed eating fish that was freshly steamed or broiled, families also freeze their catch to save for use during the winter months. Some women make fish sauce or pickle the fish in a salty brine. There has been some concern over the greater-than-average fish consumption of the Hmong compared to other Wisconsin anglers. High levels of PCB contamination in the lower Green Bay-Fox River ecosystem poses health concerns for the Hmong, especially if they are unaware (as many were) of consumption advisory reports (Hutchison and Kraft, 1994).

Hunting is usually seen as a male activity—for men of all ages—and provides many men with the opportunity to resume activities that were part of their life in Laos. During hunting season, the primary animals hunted are squirrel, deer, and game birds. There is always an air of excitement in Hmong households when men return home from hunting squirrel or other small game. As the women clean and prepare the meat, stories about the hunt are told to household members. Relatives are usually called and invited to share in eating the freshly killed meat; after the meal, the relatives are generally given a share of the uncooked meat to take home.

Men who are not working derive a sense of contentment and gratification from being able to provide for their families through hunting. Westermeyer, Neider, and Vang (1984) found that hunting and fishing activities actually contributed to improved health for some Hmong men who, since coming to the United States, were experiencing levels of psychological distress, such as anxiety and depression. The meat from hunting provides for the family above and beyond the foodstamps and AFDC that unemployed men bring in. Men also derive satisfaction when they can give meat to their brothers and other relatives. In general, kindness, generosity, and affection are commonly expressed by giving food. Although many Hmong parents rarely express physical or verbal affection towards their children, the food they provide is an expression of their love. To be able to eat whenever one is hungry is the material manifestation of parents' duties of caring for their family. This kind of love and generosity is extended to anyone who comes to visit Hmong homes, as well as to friends and relatives who may be in need.

## RAISING CHICKENS

Chicken is a favorite food in Hmong households. Families complain that the beef, pork and chicken at the grocery store does not taste good; it tastes, they say, of chemicals and additives that farmers give to their animals before they sell them. The response of some families in the Wausau area is to raise their own chickens. This was not possible in urban areas like Madison.

I met ten different families in Wausau, mostly from the C clan, who had figured out an ingenious way to raise chickens. Several clan leaders had located a retired farm woman on the outskirts of town who was willing to let them use her barn rent-free. Her only stipulation was that they keep the place clean. She also gave them free access to garden plots and the water on her land. The families were able to come and go when they liked without her permission. Besides chickens, one of the families raised ducks which were sold to the Hmong community. I was not aware of other clans raising chickens or ducks.

Chickens were raised for personal consumption and also given to relatives who came to visit. The impact of raising the chickens spread over an area much greater than Wausau. One family butchered ten chickens to send back with her mother who lived in St. Paul. Other relatives traveled to Wausau to get live chickens from the families of the C clan. The families also sold chickens to the Hmong community, thus providing a service to those families who needed live chickens for ritual and healing ceremonies or for weddings. A major complaint about buying store-bought chickens is that they do not include the head and feet, necessary parts in Hmong ritual to foretell the future.

The ability to raise their own chickens for food and ritual purposes gave those involved a sense of control over their lives and made them less dependent on others. Raising chickens, like gardening and foraging, linked "Old World" activities to the new country and reduced Hmong fears about losing their culture and about being unable to practice their religious beliefs. Although I doubt it was cheaper to raise rather than buy chickens, many Hmong felt that they no longer had to spend time trying to find sympathetic farmers willing to sell them live chickens for personal consumption.

## CONCLUSION

Gardening, hunting and gathering and, in some cases, raising chickens, are a means of subsistence for Hmong families, which also extend the families' net available cash. The activities give Hmong a sense that they are preserving their traditional culture; at the same time, they gain a sense of economic self-sufficiency. The Hmong who are dependent on welfare benefits view the subsistence activities as work, and are proud that they can feed their family and enjoy a lifestyle above and beyond what the AFDC and foodstamp allotments alone provide.

The subsistence activities also provide ways for families to maintain traditional forms of sharing and economic support, while at the same time combining work with leisure. Children are taken to the parks to play while their parents fish or forage. Foraging, when done by the whole family, is made into "fun" for the children, while teaching them the techniques and the value of traditional subsistence strategies.

The continuation of traditional subsistence activities in the United States can be seen on one level as maintaining homeland practices that provide practical solutions to the high cost of consumer goods, and offer an economic advantage for low income households. From an ecological perspective, the traditional practices capitalize on and exploit available resources not being tapped by other groups.

At yet another level, the successful application of homeland practices creates a self-conscious recognition of the Hmong's differences from other groups in the United States and reinforces their own historical image as a self-sufficient people who can survive as they have done for centuries. Despite the adversity they face as refugees and strangers in a new land, Hmong people build on their cultural differences.

Hmong attitudes about their uniqueness as a people are grounded in the emphasis they place on family and kinship ties and in the belief that they can provide for themselves and remain relatively independent of larger social and economic systems. Often, Hmong compare themselves favorably to other groups; they feel that many "Americans" lack what they have as Hmong, the ability to be frugal, to work hard, and to provide for their families.

The Hmong continually draw on the symbolic imagery of the "mother country," in which subsistence activities have become heightened markers of identity in the United States. Hmong-produced videos, the subject of the next chapter, are also important in shaping what it means to be Hmong in the United States.

# 7

# From Story Cloth to Video: Visions of the Future

**O**ne chilly morning in October, Yee invites me to her house in Wausau to observe a shaman ritual (called *ua neeb*) being held for her sick husband. The house is crowded with relatives. Children run through the living room giggling and playing. Sounds from women in the kitchen—the rhythmic chopping of vegetables and meat on wooden cutting boards—mix with the chanting sounds of the shaman. A pig's head rests on the table by the shaman. Three live chickens cackle and squirm in the nearby cardboard box. The air is thick and humid from the smoking joss sticks and the steamy pots boiling on the stove. In the living room, a group of men gather around the television set, watching a videotape filmed in Laos. They chat about the homeland as they watch New Year images flit across the screen and blend into the already noisy room.

Down the block, another Hmong family is entertaining relatives visiting from St. Paul and Fresno. A video of their family reunion is being made while, at the same time, they watch another video taken of the funeral services of a deceased relative in California.

In the late afternoon a group of female relatives gather at the oldest relative's house to talk and sew while their husbands are out hunting squirrel. One of the women plays a Hmong video filmed in Laos about a man kidnapping a bride (*zij poj niam*). They giggle and talk as they watch, reminiscing about their own courtships and marriages. They watch the video three times—with repeated rewindings of the bride capture scene—before they play a new video.

Preparing food for a shaman's healing ceremony.

In the evening another family sits in front of their television, watching a video made in India. All the children huddled close to the television set. The oldest girl, age eight, tells me: "Now watch closely. Something very funny is going to happen." She has seen the video before. She explains "This is Tarzan. He speaks Hmong and can do kung fu just like us."

## INTRODUCTION

Videos play an important part in the life of Hmong refugees in the United States.[1] Most Hmong households own a VCR or have access to one owned by a close relative; relatively few households have camcorders. Hmong, as a group, have been quick to see how VCRs and camcorders give them the means to document and, to share with others, elements of their own culture and traditions. Many Hmong fear that they will lose their "culture" now that they are in the United States. Culture for them includes traditions and customs, clothing, language, rituals, and the closeness of family and kinship ties. They value their videos, especially those about the homeland, because they consider them to be educational documents for teaching their children about Hmong ways and what it means to be Hmong.

This chapter explores a newly emerging form of narrative, the Hmong-made video, as it takes its position alongside a more traditional Hmong form of visual expression, the *paj ntaub*, or story cloth. I examine the social context of these home videos, their social function in Hmong family and community, and their representational nature in terms of how the Hmong socially construct their past, their homeland, their culture, and their traditions on film. Hmong videos give us insight into how the Hmong are adapting and adjusting to the United States, and how they perceive themselves and their place within the fabric of U.S. culture.

## STORY CLOTH

Upon arriving at Chia's house one evening I was surprised by the presence of three pieces of Hmong needlework hanging in a row across the living room wall. The outer two pieces consisted of geometric appliquéd designs while the center piece was an embroidered picture, a story cloth (*paj ntaub*) depicting Hmong village life. I moved closer to examine the story cloth. "My country," Ying said in Hmong, pointing to the scene in which, in the foreground, Hmong people were walking single file up a winding road carrying baskets of rice, wood, and corn on their backs. Several men on horseback rode in front of the group, leading them back to the village. Several houses represented the village and were surrounded by the activities of farm life—chickens pecking for food, pigs feeding at a trough, young girls grinding corn, and boys playing with tops. Mountains loomed in the background.

Ying started her story of the cloth with a broad sweep of the whole picture stating, "My family, we did like this. We were farmers like this in Laos." It didn't take her long, however, to move into the minute details of her life, as if the intricate stitches in the cloth required the storyteller to speak in the same threaded way:

> Every day I got up early, before the sun. I got up when the roosters start their cry. I fed the chickens, carried the water, worked the fields. These girls grinding corn, I used to do just like this too. It is very hard work but we were healthy.

Ying traced the road with her fingertips, pointing to the corn fields, the ripening rice, and the squashes growing in the gardens. She began to shorten her story by calling out only the names of these things in Hmong. And then, just as quickly as the story began, she fell silent. Ying and her family arrived in the United States in 1980. They came as refugees from Laos. Ying misses her country and refers to it fondly in conversations.

Not all story cloths are of farm settings nor do they evoke such nostalgic remembrance of the homeland. Many story cloths portray the Hmong's grueling and often tragic events of escape from their homeland. Although each tapestry is unique, common themes and images appear over and over again. There are images of people fleeing with their children and their pack animals; their deadly encounter with enemy soldiers who fire on them and kill their relatives; and their desperate escape across the Mekong river to safety. The embroidered images of the story cloths document the collective experience of the group. Within the details of the collective voice, however, lie more personal and individual accounts of escape, accounts which give testimony to personal tragedies, which put faces and names to all the people silently sewn into place on the tapestry, and which tell of the needless pain, suffering, and loss of individuals and their families due to war.

## HMONG VIDEOS

*Paj ntaub* is the Hmong word for flower cloth (or as those in the United States have come to know it, "story cloth"), an embroidery art form that has decorated Hmong clothing for centuries and that serves as an identifying marker for individual clans, subgroups, and regions. *Paj ntaub* has changed radically since 1975, from symmetrical and geometric designs to pictorial images reflecting stylized themes of traditional Hmong life in Laos as well as their tragic exodus after the fall of the government to the Pathet Lao Communist forces.

The pictorial narratives in the *paj ntaub* story cloth have their origins in the refugee camps. Hmong-made videos take root in the United States. Both are forms of visual communication about Hmong history, culture, and traditions. However, they differ fundamentally in their representation of what it means to be Hmong. The embroidered story cloths have been created to capitalize on a consumer market to raise money while in refugee camps. Because *paj ntaub* makes a public statement about the Hmong for the Other, certain themes and subject matter are rarely reflected in the story cloth (i.e. cultivation of opium poppy, funerals, or U.S. soldiers and personnel in Laos during the Vietnam era) (Peterson, 1988).

Unlike the story cloth, the Hmong videos are created solely for a Hmong audience. The videos are therefore a means for the Hmong to look at themselves without worrying about the criticism of non-Hmong consumers and market demands.

As I visited Hmong homes and watched the videos circulate within the community, I realized that the videos had value beyond their entertainment and preservation functions. They provided a cultural backdrop and climate for talking about the past, the present, and the future. The videos facilitated conversation about Hmong culture and life in Laos and also brought forth opinions about life in the United States and the differences between Hmong and U.S. culture.

## CATEGORIES OF HMONG VIDEOS

I have categorized the Hmong-made videos into three different types—"home-mode" videos, Hmong-made commercial videos, and Asian feature videos dubbed in Hmong. Commercial videos include what I call homeland videos, drama and re-enactment videos, and beauty-pageant videos.

Home-mode videos document family life and community events. There are videos of family gatherings, picnics, birthday parties, vacations, Sunday outings to the park, soccer and volleyball games, church parties, shamanic rituals, weddings, New Year's celebrations, and funerals. The videos document occasions that have meaning and importance to Hmong families, and they are usually shared only within the context and confines of the family home or with close clan members. People watch these videos mainly as news, documents for family members who may not have been present to participate in the events. Home-mode videos have an added benefit; not only do they provide the means for communicating and sharing group events, but also a way for geographically separated families to maintain and strengthen kinship ties and group affliation, irrespective of place, time, or distance.

Commercial videos are produced by Hmong people who intend to sell them to other interested Hmong (irrespective of kinship affiliation). The most popular and frequently viewed videos are homeland videos which are produced with a more general Hmong audience in mind. The videos are made by amateur Hmong filmmakers who go to the homeland (either Thailand, Laos, or China) as tourists. Upon returning home, they prepare and market the videos they have made, distributing them through kinship channels to Hmong communities throughout the United States, thus reimbursing themselves for their trip.

While documenting places they visit on their vacations, these amateur filmmakers consciously attempt to document many facets of Hmong culture in the homeland. Since many Hmong return to the homeland for the Hmong New Year, New Year celebrations are the main focus of many of these videos.

Various patterns in thematic material surface in the homeland videos. Like the *paj ntaub* story cloth, homeland videos display the land, animals, agricultural cycles, and cultural practices of the Hmong. Distant shots of mountains are combined with the sound of traditional musical instruments that are a signal to the audience that "this is Hmong." The narrator then guides the viewers on a pilgrimage to their homeland and their past.

Similar to the intricate stitches required in a *paj ntaub* story cloth, the details in the homeland videos are put together in ethnographic fashion to make as complete a record of the Hmong lifestyle as possible. Filmmakers focus attention on the types of crops being grown and on the condition of fields, houses, villages, and clothing. Shots of farm tools and machinery are never shown in isolation; there is always a person using them. Work scenes reflect men and women's gender roles and children's duties, and provide viewers with a general feeling of what life is like in a Hmong village or community. The audience watches, using these categories and images to connect to their past, often making comments and judgments about life in the homeland.

It is not uncommon to find Hmong families playing homeland videos throughout the day as entertainment. They put them into the VCR when relatives visit or when they are resting or sewing. Sometimes they play these videotapes several times during the course of a day. The videos recreate the sights and sounds of homeland village life within the living room. The scenes thus serve as a backdrop, or landscape, for their daily lives.

The social context for viewing homeland videos is one of "communal re-creation" as participants recall, re-experience, and share their pasts with the group. For instance, images of mountains and fields spurred one woman in her late fifties to recall a time in Laos when she was sixteen years old. She was given her own plot of opium to farm in order to earn money to make her New Year clothing. Another woman in her late twenties compared her life in the United States to her childhood in Laos while watching a homeland video which showed three young Hmong girls in Laos, each about eight years old, sewing their own clothes. The image evoked the following response from this woman:

> I cannot see my own daughter [age eight] doing that. She doesn't seem old enough to make her own clothes like those girls. She would not be able to do it. I'm not sure that I could do it anymore either. I used to sew everything, but now I'm not sure I want to. It takes a lot of time. I do not have a lot of time like that anymore. I am just too busy.

The woman's daughter pipes in: "Mommy I couldn't do it either," and then proceeds to ask questions about the homeland, as many of the younger children do, continually reminding the adults of the old and new. "Mommy, did you even have lemonade there?" or "What was it like without a bathroom?," or "Is it cold at night without a furnace?" Yet many teens and college-age youths find the homeland videos boring and do not understand why their parents and relatives watch these videos so often. One twenty year-old student, home on a college break, said to me "I've seen this video so many times I can watch it with my eyes closed."

Homeland videos elaborate on various topics such as the cultivation and harvesting of opium and images of war. Those focused on war provoke numerous comments from Hmong men. In one video, a countryside that was once heavily forested is now bare because, as one man commented to me, "all the American bombs destroyed the trees." Another man watching the same video commented that the empty bomb casings, shown stacked up in the middle of one village, are "like a war memorial." While most of the men's comments reflect regret, one Hmong man remembered the bombing raids in Laos differently. He told me how he creatively used the bombings to his advantage:

> We all knew that they [Americans] would bomb anything that looked like a village. I saw the big craters left by the bombs and how they would fill up with water after the rains. I thought to myself: "this would make a good fish

pond if only I could get one closer to my home." So I went out one day and hung a lot of old clothes out on the trees and on the ground. It was only a matter of days and I had myself my own fish pond.

Homeland videos also serve as progress reports about the homeland. The conditions evident in images of the material environment indicate to viewers the economic well-being of a particular village and the homeland in general. The tiniest details are scrutinized for clues that provide information on conditions of life in Laos. I have heard viewers make general comments such as: "The people are poorer now, you can tell by the roofs of their houses; we never let our houses go like that," or "Their clothes are not good; the children do not look healthy." Yet, for many older Hmong, the homeland looks good. One woman in her fifties comments:

> When my family watches this video, we think we were crazy to come to this country [America]. When we see the video we want to go back. It still looks pretty good to us. And we think we would not have to be minorities like we are here, in this country.[2]

The homeland videos also have the potential to create visions of a future. At one extended family gathering, the men began arguing about the possibility of returning to Laos while watching a homeland video. One young man in his early thirties commented:

> I would like to start some sort of hotel business in Laos. Then the Hmong from America could stay there while they were visiting. But I am not sure about the economy there. Perhaps everything is still too shaky right now.

Many Hmong women felt differently from their husbands about returning to the homeland. Women, generally up to the age of forty-five, stated they would not go back because of the improvements in their life style and living conditions here. One woman put it succinctly:

> We [women] have it much better here in America. We have running water in our houses, so that our work is not as hard here. We can take our clothes to the laundromat. There is plenty of food and refrigerators to keep the flies off the meat. And there are doctors and hospitals so that

our children do not get sick and die. I do not want to go back.

Homeland videos also provide a catalyst for dialogue among Hmong about their identity as a people, both locally and globally. Julia Dobrow found that when members of ethnic groups watched ethnic videos, the experience provided "a forum for defining and reinforcing ethnic affiliation, and differences between themselves and the host society," as well as a way to achieve social solidarity (1989: 204). This seems true for Hmong as well. Whenever I have watched homeland videos with Hmong families, they have always made a point of telling me that "this is our culture, this is the way we used to do everything. We had no cars, or machines. We worked hard like this." Some viewers relate work to the family and say things such as: "Our families all help each other, just like this. Americans, they don't do this. They tell their children to 'leave home' when they turn eighteen, but we take care of our children. We help them. We work together."

U.S. Hmong also use homeland videos to compare themselves to the Hmong living in Thailand, Laos, and China. From comments made by viewers watching the homeland videos, I sensed that, for U.S. Hmong, the homeland Hmong are becoming the Other, "like us but not like us." Some comments I have heard about this Other are positive and reflect a lowering of self-esteem since coming to the United States. Women make statements such as: "They are prettier than the Hmong in the United States. They look natural in their dresses and they don't need to wear makeup like the Hmong in America." On one occasion a young man in his twenties, watching a homeland video filmed in China, commented:

> The Chinese Hmong don't look like Hmong. We have left China over 200 years ago, and so we have changed a lot from them. They even speak a little different from us. But I sure like the way she [a young unmarried girl] sings. She is very beautiful.

During a viewing of another homeland video, a Hmong teenage girl commented about her uncle's trip to the homeland: "My uncle told me you can't trust them, even though they are our relatives. They might just kill you and take your money when you aren't looking."

At the same time, many U.S. Hmong regard the homeland Hmong as impoverished, uneducated, and lacking sophistication of the wider world, a world in which U.S. Hmong now live. Several men I talked with felt that U.S. Hmong know so much more now than Laotian Hmong that they actually could help Laos prosper if they could return. One man told me:

> Even the least educated American Hmong would be able to get a better job than the Hmong in Laos. We have learned a lot from being in America. We know more now. I think we could do very well if we returned.

A Hmong businessman from St. Paul who was visiting one of my informants commented that, although homeland videos get U.S. Hmong excited about returning to Laos, "If the Hmong go back to Laos, they must go back fully educated so that they can take over and rule the country. They cannot go back just to be farmers again."

The videos often include Hmong from Thailand and Laos talking directly to the Hmong in the United States. They say things like, "Please come back. You know so much now; you will be able to help us," and "Come and marry our sons and daughters."

Another subcategory of commercial videos consists of those filmed either in the homeland or in the United States that portray, in dramatic form, some aspect of Hmong history, culture, traditions, or romantic conflicts. These I term drama and reenactment videos. Unlike homeland videos, drama and reenactment videos are popular with teenagers. These videos have brought teens back into the living room with their families. Some common themes in these videos include the re-enactment of a family's escape from Laos (filmed in a forested area of Minnesota along the St. Croix River, which audiences recognize as the Mekong); the kidnapping of a bride (in which various Hmong audiences were confused about whether the incident was "real" or "just pretend"); and the life of an orphan boy in Laos (a prevalent theme in Hmong folktales).

Other drama videos dwell on issues that are particularly relevant for young marriageable Hmong men and women. Love stories, stories of failed marriages, and stories focusing on the problems of polygyny and infertility are some of the themes enacted in "soap opera" fashion, with all the accouterments of upper middle-class U.S. lifestyle as reflected on television. Some drama videos draw on basic themes found in Hmong folktales (see Johnson, 1985), but place them within the context of contemporary life in the United States. Protagonists are always well educated and rich and, for the most part, the stories have a happy ending.

Another type of commercial video made by Hmong is the beauty pageant video. These incorporate actual film footage of Hmong beauty contests, showing the selection of "Miss Hmong" in a particular state. The principal states where Hmong host "Miss Hmong" pageants are California, Wisconsin, Minnesota, and Michigan, all states with large Hmong populations. Beauty pageant videos can be rented or purchased; the latest "Miss Hmong" videos are usually available from local Hmong ethnic food stores. The young marriageable women who participate in these events gain national reputations in Hmong communities. The selection process also reflects broader internal issues of clan politics.

Finally, several Hmong producers of homeland videos now translate and dub various Asian-made video soundtracks into Hmong, making a more meaningful text for Hmong viewers. Hmong do not usually purchase these videos but rather rent them from the local ethnic food store; favorites are sometimes copied and circulated among kinship networks for extended viewing. The most popular Asian feature videos are action-oriented videos in which the characters are of Asian origin, or in which the action takes place within a landscape similar to the homeland. Many of these videos are produced in India, Thailand, the Phillipines, and Hong Kong, and favorites feature love and adventure stories containing kung fu heroes, princes, kings, and paupers.

## CONCLUSION

Homeland videos serve as archives and re-creations of Hmong life and history in the United States and the homeland, as progress reports on the homeland, and as vehicles that promote dialogue with other Hmong around the world. Facilitated by technological advances like VCRs and computers, this dialogue has the potential to create a sense of solidarity and ethnic identity among peoples at a transnational level, irrespective of place or geography. Asian feature videos, as well as homeland videos, also bring a piece of the homeland into the privacy of one's home. While viewing these tapes, Hmong can renew their sense of being part of a community and leave behind the sense of being a minority, or outcast, in their new surroundings. These videos reinforce positive elements of ethnic identity and collective continuity and belonging.

Sense of place and a sense of belonging are crucial concepts that come into play when we study people who have lost a home(land), such as the Hmong and other refugees. People react to the loss of their homes with grief—grief that is intensified by a host of factors: the fragmentation of routines and relationships, changes in expectations, loss of objects, fragmentation of spatial-ly-oriented actions, and disruption of one's sense of continuity with the past, the present, and the future (Fried, 1963: 153).

Hmong videos (especially homeland videos) give Hmong viewers the opportunity not only to recall people who have been significant in their lives, but also to reconcile and realign their sense of place as well. Thus, by providing strategies for working through new meanings of space and place, and for continuity and belonging in the United States, the Hmong videos may very well be indicators of health and healing in the grieving process for a group having lost a homeland.

Finally these videos help us understand how Hmong are adapting and adjusting to the United States, and how they see themselves and their place within the fabric of U.S. culture. The Hmong videos show that Hmong are a creative, enterprising, and future-oriented group. Even the most recent drama and reenact-ment videos portray Hmong who have achieved educational, oc-cupational, and material success in the United States.

The Hmong videos suggest new directions for looking at how immigrants and refugees express and represent themselves and their world on film. The videos are a legitimate and significant form of voice in which ordinary people "write" their own history and culture (Clifford & Marcus, 1986) and, perhaps, through their own "writing," take control of the future they see for themselves in the United States.

## NOTES

1. A published version of this chapter "Telling Narratives through Home Videos: Hmong Refugees and Self-Documentation of Life in the Old and New Country" appears in the *Journal of American Folklore*, Vol. 106(422): 435–449.

2. This is a curious remark because Hmong were considered a minority group in Laos too. In Laos their separateness is defined by cultural characteristics, whereas in the United States, many Hmong feel that their separateness is defined by physical characteristics such as skin and hair coloring. This is understandable in rural Wisconsin, where one finds predominantly white, European ethnic communities.

# 8

# Conclusion

An article in the "Wausau Hmong American News," a quarterly newsletter published by the Wausau Area Hmong Mutual Association, noted the twentieth anniversary of the date the first Hmong family arrived in Wausau—April 9, 1976. As of April, 1996 there were 650 Hmong families residing in Wausau or about 4,500 people. The article noted that homeownership was also up. Currently, there are about 250 homes in the Wausau area owned by Hmong families, as well as various Hmong-owned businesses. Over 700 Hmong are working full time and many others have part-time jobs. More than 300 area Hmong students have completed high school, seventy-five are currently attending college, and sixty individuals have completed their college education. About 50 percent of the students graduating from high school go on to technical and vocational schools. Many of the graduates have returned to the Wausau area as engineers, school counselors, teachers, nurses, police officers, social workers, computer programers, and businessmen (P. Yang, 1996: 7).

## DISPELLING ANTI-IMMIGRANT RHETORIC

An article appearing in *The Atlantic Monthly* entitled "The Ordeal of Immigration in Wausau" (Beck, 1994a: 84) starts out by stating:

> Since 1970 the majority of population growth in the United States has come from immigrants and their direct descendants. Demographers predict that this trend will intensify in the new century if federal laws remain unchanged. For a look at a possible American future, consider the fate of a small midwestern city [Wausau].

Roy Beck's article then proceeds to blame the Hmong for all the social and economic troubles facing Wausau today, among them burgeoning school enrollments and overcrowded facilities, increased public welfare receipt and unemployment, overburdened native taxpayers, gang violence, and the inability of newcomers to assimilate into U.S. culture. One rebuttal to this article states that Beck's underlying message is "that immigrants, particularly if they are racially or culturally different, corrode our [American] way of life and therefore should be kept out" (Griswold, 1994: 6). Beck's reply was that "no matter how positive and even heroic the individual immigrants or how good the intentions of everybody connected to them, the community-wide effects can be negative (Beck, 1994b: 9).

In the popular press, Peter Brimelow (1992 and 1995), also noted for his anti-immigration views, argues that under current immigration policy, the United States is heading for a disastrous future. He notes that by the year 2050, one-third of the United States's nearly 400 million people will be made up of post-1970 immigrants and their descendants. He claims that, currently, many of these new immigrants are disportionately prone to poverty, crime and welfare dependency because U.S. immigration policy is focused on family reunification, rather than job skills (1992: 32). With today's welfare system, Brimelow argues that "the failures are no longer winnowed out. Instead, they are encouraged to stay—at the expense of the American taxpayer" (Brimelow, 1995). Brimelow concludes from the evidence that the "relative lack of skills among the post-1965 immigrants seems likely to be repeated among their children" (1995: 55) and hence implies that, in the future, there will be a continued cycle of poverty, crime, and welfare use among these immigrant groups.

Labels such as "refugees," "welfare recipients," "illiterate," and "uneducated," create powerful images such as helplessness, dependency, and tax burden, and may actually blind us to the actual situation at hand. Immigrant success or failure has much to do with family, with the community context, the prejudice that immigrants face, and the structure of opportunities available to new immigrant groups (Portes and Zhou, 1993: 76). Portes and Zhou point out that greater family cohesiveness may contribute to successful second-generation education outcomes (1993: 80), especially if the youths remain within their ethnic community which can provide the material and social capital for educational and economic advancement (Portes and Zhou, 1993: 81–82). They also note that if second-generation children are exposed to marginalized sub-cultures of native youths then, "Assimilation may not be into maintream values and expectations but into the adversarial stance of impoverished groups confined to the bottom of the economic hourglass" (Portes and Zhou, 1993: 85).

When attention is turned to the domestic domain of Hmong households in Wausau, one finds that the family provides the emotional and psychological reference point for combatting loneliness and alienation as well as a place and purpose for its members (Kivisto, 1990: 473). Families are the main locus for social life, providing links to employment, services, and knowledge about the wider outside world and the ethnic community. Examining various Hmong family budgets, spending and saving behaviors, and their selective acceptance of consumer goods, leads one to conclude that Hmong families are concerned about their future economic situation and that they do not view it as grimly as Roy Beck or Peter Brimelow.

There is no doubt that education is a must for successful immigrants in a post-industrial world, and the Hmong indeed present an interesting paradox in the anti-immigration discourse of Beck and Brimelow. The majority of Hmong, as noted in earlier chapters, have come to the United States with little or no education, training or job skills. Yet Hmong students today are going on to college and higher education in record numbers. Some are first generation refugees while others are U.S.-born. Almost all of these graduates are going on to white collar jobs and moving into middle income status.

National data comparing the educational success of Indochinese refugee children show some surprising results as well. The Cambodian and Lao students had the lowest average of GPAs and test scores in comparison to the Vietnamese and Chinese refugees, who ranked highest of the groups. The Hmong scores fell in between. Hmong data were surprising because first generation Hmong parents have less education than those in the other refugee groups (Rumbaut, 1991: 82–84).

What are the reasons for this massive push by Hmong families to educate their sons and daughters? Partly it is a result of the historical situation which thrust the Hmong into refugee status in the first place. Their experiences in war, in leadership roles and positions of power as minorities within Laos exposed them to the instrumental value of education. Initial exposure to educational opportunities was initiated in the relocation camps in Laos where, for the first time, formal schooling was available for the majority of Hmong children (Quincy, 1988: 183). After the war, however, strong clan leadership in the United States guided families towards avenues of success. Understanding that there is an ever "widening gap between the minimally paid menial jobs" and the "high-tech and professional occupations requiring college degrees" (Portes and Zhou 1993: 77), Hmong families are encouraging their children to seek higher education and white collar jobs. The payoff is that not only will the children pull their families out of welfare, but also education will be considered as the means of maintaining strong leaders within the Hmong community and maintaining Hmong collective identity in the future. It should be noted as well, that political refugees have been eligible for a variety of government programs and education loans for their children. The Cuban refugees took full advantage of these benefits which, today, is reflected in the high proportions of professional and executives among Cuban Americans (Portes and Zhou, 1993: 85). The Hmong are similarly taking advantage of educational benefits and their efforts also seem promising.

While Hmong youth are going on to higher education, many of their parents and siblings continue to remain on welfare assistance. This presents yet another paradox. Yet as I have shown, Hmong families perceive and utilize welfare in distinctive ways. Welfare and the programs that go along with needs-based assistance are viewed by most Hmong as a resource to be exploited in order to meet the challenges of improving their economic life in the United States in the short term.

Although many Hmong families work for low wages and the Hmong population has high unemployment rates nationwide, we do not see what Oscar Lewis (1965: xlii) has termed a "culture of poverty" among them. Hmong do not have a present-time orientation, low aspirations, feelings of fatalism, inferiority, passivity, resignation or mother-centered households. Hmong families are characterized by values that prize self-sufficiency, saving and thrift, hard work, goal-setting, delayed gratification, future orientation, independence, and an emphasis on strong family ties and kinship cooperation, from the smallest social unit of the household (*tsev neeg*) all the way up to the largest unit of the clan (*xeem*). This system of values and social organization gives individuals a sense of identity and belonging, and influences the types of choices and decisions that individuals and families make economically.[1]

For the Hmong, upward mobility for a single individual means that one's family will follow. Diversification of income and resources within the Hmong family, as I pointed out, have produced a greater cash flow than is possible with a single income wage earner. Non-working adult members provide vital functions of childcare as well as traditional subsistence activities which further enhance savings. And the fact is that Hmong kinship networks are not bound by locality. Mobility and distance do not disrupt the responsibilities and obligations of members within the kinship network. With the convenience of modern communication and transportation networks, families stay in touch nationally and transnationally, and provide one another with social, psychological, and economic support. The most important aspect of maintaining networks is that there are resources that can flow through them.

Through thrift and selective consumption, Hmong families are able to save. Food reserves, found in the family freezer and storage rooms, are the visible markers of the family's frugality, wealth and well-being. Many Hmong also have the ability to "stretch the dollar." This is connected to a sound understanding of capitalism and principles of economic and business practices. Indeed, many Hmong are exceptionally astute in knowing how to spend money in ways that actually earn them more. The Hmong have been able to selectively purchase consumer goods which serve as symbolic markers of middle-class status. These goods represent prosperity and stability, and also provide a means for the Hmong to participate in American life.

The Hmong easily incorporate the newest technologies into their own lifestyles, especially those which sustain and facilitate Hmong social networks and maintain Hmong cultural practices, traditions, and identities. Telephone conversations, and audio and video cassette recordings have actually narrowed the distance between their homeland and their new land by providing constant and sometimes instant feedback and commentary on the events happening locally and globally. Hmong videos travel through kinship and clan networks, moving images and ideas across multiple Hmong diaspora communities, and thus, create a complex transnational dialogue between the Hmong in the United States and those in Laos, Thailand, China, and elsewhere.

Emergent forms of U.S. cultural activities and holidays such as picnics, birthday parties, Father's and Mother's Day, Independence Day, Thanksgiving, and Christmas are being fitted into Hmong lifestyles and identities, especially as these forms relate to kinship networks. U.S. holidays and celebrations combine with folk celebrations and incorporate elements from both a traditional Hmong past and a modern U.S. present. One might speak of them as unfolding dramas rather than rituals (Bodnar, 1985: 186), for they are uniquely adaptive and changing; they create a celebratory mood in which to display, edit, interpret, and transform the past identity of Hmongness while, at the same time, they help to define present and future identities.

With continued media coverage eager to report conflict between immigrants and established residents, we need to ask "What is happening in the quiet, day-to-day activities that the media never examine[s]?"(Bach, 1993: 159). When we ask this question we realize that Roy Beck's (1994a) and Peter Brimelow's (1992 and 1995) anti-immigration rhetoric reflects an argument that is detached from the human element involved in immigration. They tell us little about the actual lives of immigrants, the struggles they are facing, and the success stories. They simplify the issues by ignoring or underestimating the forces of assimilation and the eagerness of immigrants to adopt U.S. values as their own (Bernstein, 1995). What seems clear from this study is that the Hmong exhibit a willingness to take a chance, embracing change as an opportunity in order to pursue the American dream.

## NOTES

1. Oscar Lewis notes that "Wherever there are unilateral kinship systems or clans one would not expect to find the culture of poverty, because a clan system gives people a sense of belonging to a corporate body with a history and a life of its own, thereby providing a sense of continuity, a sense of a past and of a future" (Lewis, 1965: xlix).

# References

Adams, Nina S. and Afred W. McCoy (eds.)
1970    Laos: War and Revolution. New York: Torchbook Library Edition, Harper and Row.

Appadurai, Arjun
1991    Global Ethnoscapes: Notes and Queries for a Transnational Anthropology in *Recapturing Anthropology: Working in the Present*. Richard G. Fox (ed.). (pp. 191–210.) New Mexico: School of American Research Press.

Bach, Robert L.
1988    State Intervention in Southeast Asian Refugee Resettlement in the United States, *Journal of Refugee Studies* 1 (1), 38–56.
1993    Recrafting the Common Good: Immigration and Community, *The Annals of the American Academy of Political and Social Sciences*, November, 155–170.

Bach, Robert L. and Rita Carroll-Seguin
1986    Labor Force Participation, Household Composition, and Sponsorship Among Southeast Asian Refugees, *International Migration Review* 20 (2), 381–404.

Baer, Florence
1982    Give Me...Your Huddled Masses: Anti-Vietnamese Refugee Lore and the "Image of Limited Good," *Western Folklore 41*, 275–291.

Barney, G. Linwood
1967    The Meo of Xieng Khouang Province, Laos in *Southeast Asian Tribes, Minorities, and Nations*. Vol. I, Peter Kunstadter (ed.). (pp. 271–294.) Princeton, NJ: Princeton University Press.
1980    The Hmong of Northern Laos in *Glimpses of Hmong History and Culture*. Indochinese Refugee Education Guides, #16. (pp. 18–44.) Washington, DC: National Indochinese Clearinghouse, Center for Applied Linguistics.

Beck, Roy
1994a   The Ordeal of Immigration in Wausau, *The Atlantic Monthly 273* (4):84–97.
1994b   Letters to the Editor: Hmong in Wausau, *The Altlantic Monthly 273* (7), 6–9.

Bernatzik, Hugo
1970    *Akha and Miao: Problems of Applied Ethnography in Farther India* (Alois Nagler, Trans.). New Haven: Human Relations Area File. (Original work published 1947)

Bernstein, Richard
   1995   The Immigration Wave: A Plea to Hold it Back, Book Review of Alien
          Nation by Peter Brimelow. *New York Times*, section B2, April 19.

Bodnar, John
   1985   *The Transplanted: A History of Immigrants in Urban America.* Bloomington:
          Indiana University Press.

Brimelow, Peter
   1992   Time to Rethink Immigration? *National Review*, June 22, 1992, pp. 30–46.
   1995   *Alien Nation: Common Sense About America's Immigration Disaster.* New
          York: Random House.

Caplan, Nathan; John K. Whitmore, and Quang L. Bui
   1985   *Southeast Asian Refugee Self-Sufficiency Study.* Washington DC: Office of
          Refugee Resettlement. U.S. Dept. of Health and Human Services.

Caplan, Nathan; John K. Whitmore, and Marcella Choy
   1989   *The Boat People and Achievement in America: A Study of Economic and Educ-
          tional Success.* Ann Arbor: University of Michigan Press.

Chan, Sucheng (ed.)
   1994   *Hmong Means Free:Life in Laos and America.* Philadelphia:Temple Univer-
          sity Press.

Chindarsi, Nusit
   1976   *The Religion of the Hmong Njua.* Bangkok: The Siam Society.

Chun, K. and A. Deinard
   1986   Undue Lead Absorption in Hmong Children in *The Hmong in Transition.*
          Glenn Hendricks et.al (eds.). (pp. 417–425.) New York and Minneapolis:
          Center for Migration Studies and Southeast Asian Refugee Studies, Uni-
          versity of Minnesota.

Clifford, James and George E. Marcus (eds.)
   1986   *Writing Culture: The Poetics and Politics of Ethnography.* Berkeley: Universi-
          ty of California Press.

Cohen, Anthony
   1985   *The Symbolic Construction of Community.* New York: Tavistock.

Cohen, Erik
   1989   International Politics and the Transformation of Folkcrafts—The Hmong
          (Meo) of Thailand and Laos, *The Journal of the Siam Society* 77, 69–82.

Cohn, Mary et.al
   1984   *The Hmong Resettlement Study Site Report: Orange County California.* Sub-
          mitted by Northwest Regional Educational Laboratory, Portland,
          Oregon to Office of Refugee Resettlement, Washington, DC.

Conquergood, Dwight
   1988   Health Theatre in a Hmong Refugee Camp: Performance, Communica-
          tion, and Culture, *The Drama Review* 32 (3), 174–208.

Cooper, Robert, Nicholas Tapp, Garry Yia Lee, and Gretel Schwoer-Kohl
   1991   *The Hmong.* Bankok, Thailand: ArtAsia Press Co. LTD.

Daniels, Roger
   1990   *Coming to America: A History of Immigration and Ethnicity in American Life.*
          New York: Harper Collins.

Des Pres, Terrence
1976    *The Survivor: An Anatomy of Life in the Death Camps.* New York: Oxford University Press.

Dobrow, Julia R.
1989    Away from the Mainstream? VCRs and Ethnic Identity in *The VCR Age: Home Video and Mass Communication.* Mark R. Levy (ed.). (pp. 193–208.) Newbury Park, CA: Sage Pub.

Donnelly, Nancy D.
1986    Factors Contributing to a Split Within a Clientelistic Needlework Cooperative Engaged in Refugee Resettlement in *The Hmong in Transition.* Glenn L. Hendricks et.al (eds.). (pp. 159–173.) New York and Minnesota: Center for Migration Studies and Southeast Asian Refugee Studies of the University of Minnesota.
1994    *Changing Lives of Refugee Hmong Women.* Seattle: University of Washington Press.

Downing, Bruce T.
1984a   *The Hmong Resettlement Study Site Report: Dallas-Fort Worth, Texas.* Submitted by Northwest regional Educational Laboratory, Portland, Oregon to Office of Refugee Resettlement, Washington, DC.
1984b   *The Hmong Resettlement Study Site Report: Fort Smith, Arkansas.* Submitted by Northwest Regional Educational Laboratory, Portland, Oregon to Office of Refugee Resettlement, Washington, DC.
1984c   *The Hmong Resettlement Study Site Report: Minneapolis-St. Paul.* Submitted by Northwest Regional Educational Laboratory, Portland, Oregon to the Office of Refugee Resettlement, Washington, DC.

Dunnigan, Timothy
1982    Segmentary Kinship in an Urban Society: The Hmong of St. Paul-Minneapolis, *Anthropological Quarterly 55*, 126–134.

Dunnigan, Timothy and Douglas P. Olney
1985    "Hmong" in *Refugees in the United States: A Reference Handbook.* David W. Haines (ed.). (pp. 111–126.) Westport, Conn: Greenwood Press.

Fass, Simon
1991    *The Hmong in Wisconsin: On the Road to Self-Sufficiency.* Milwaukee, WI: The Wisconsin Policy Research Institute, Vol.4 (2).

Fass, Simon M. and Diane D. Bui
1984    *The Hmong Resettlement Study: Vol.II. Economic Development and Employment Projects.* Submitted by Northwest Regional Educational Laboratory, Portland, Oregon to the Office of Refugee Resettlement, Washington, DC.

Finck, John
1984    *The Hmong Resettlement Study Site Report: Providence,Rhode Island.* Submitted by Northwest Regional Educational Laboratory, Portland Oregon to the Office of Refugee Resettlement, Washington, DC.

Fink, J. and Doua Yang
1983    Peace Has not Been Made: A Case History of a Hmong Family's Encounter with a Hospital. Color video, 25 min. Rhode Island Office of Refugee Resettlement. 600 New London Ave, Cranston, RI.

Fried, Marc
1963    Grieving for a Lost Home, in *The Urban Condition: People and Policy in the Metropolis*. Leonard J. Duhl (ed.). (pp. 151–171.) New York: Basic Books.

Geddes, William R.
1976    *Migrants of the Mountains: The Cultural Ecology of the Blue Miao of Thailand*. Oxford: Clarendon Press.

Gordon, Linda W.
1989    National Surveys of Southeast Asian Refugees: Methods, Findings, Issues in *Refugees as Immigrants: Cambodians, Laotians, and Vietnamese in America*. David W. Haines (ed). (pp. 24–39.) New Jersey: Rowman and Littlefield.

Griswold, Jack
1994    Letters to the Editor: Hmong in Wausau, *The Atlantic Monthly* 273 (7), 6–8, July 1994.

Gupta, Akhil and James Ferguson
1992    Beyond 'Culture' Space, Identity, and the Politics of Difference, *Cultural Anthropology* 7 (1), 6–23.

Haines, David W.
1982    Southeast Asian Refugees in the United States: The Interaction of Kinship and Public Policy, *Anthropological Quarterly* 55 (3), 170–181.
1985    Towards Integration into American Society in *Refugees in the United States: A Reference Handbook*. David W. Haines (ed). (pp. 37–55.) Westport, CT: Greenwood Press.

Helmreich, Stefan
1992    Kinship, Nation, and Paul Gilroy's Concept of Diaspora, *Diaspora 2* (2), 243–249.

Hutchinson, Ray
1992    *Acculturation in the Hmong Community*. Wisconsin: Center for Public Affairs (University of Wisconsin-Green Bay) and Race and Ethnicity (University of Wisconsin-Milwaukee).

Hutchison, Ray and Clifford Kraft
1994    "Hmong Fishing Activity and Fish Consumption." *Journal of Great Lakes Research 20*, No. 2, 471–478.

It Pays to Stay on Welfare, Study finds. (1993, May 17). *The Janesville Gazette*, p. 1A.

Johnson, Charles (ed.)
1985    *Dab Neeg Hmoob: Myths, Legends, and Folktales from the Hmong of Laos*. St. Paul, MN: Linguistic Department, MacAlester College.

Keller, Stephen L.
1975    *Uprooting and Social Change: The Role of Refugees in Development*. New Delhi: Manohar Book Service.

Kibria, Nazli
1993    *Family Tightrope: The Changing Lives of Vietnamese Americans*. Princeton: Princeton University Press.

Kirshenblatt-Gimblett, Barbara
1983    "Studying Immigrant and Ethnic Folklore" in *Handbook of American Folklore*. Richard M. Dorson (ed.). (pp. 39–47). Bloomington: Indiana University Press.

Kivisto, Peter
1990    The Transplanted Then and Now: The Reorientation of Immigration
Studies from the Chicago School to the New Social History, *Ethnic and
Racial Studies 13* (4), 455–481.

Koltyk, Jo Ann
1993    Telling Narratives Through Home Videos: Hmong Refugees and Self-
Documentation of Life in the Old and New Country, *Journal of American
Folklore 106* (422), 435–449.

Kunz, E. F.
1973    The Refugee in Flight: Kinetic Models and Forms of Displacement, *International Migration Review 7* (2), 125–146.

Langer, Lawrence L.
1991    *Holocaust Testimonies: The Ruins of Memory.* New Haven: Yale University
Press.

Lemoine, Jacques
1972    *Un village Hmong Vert du haut Laos.* Paris, France: Centre National de la
Recherche Scientifique.

Lewis, Oscar
1965    *La Vida: A Puerto Rican Family in the Culture of Poverty.* New York:
Random House.

Lifton, Robert
1967    *Death in Life: Survivors of Hiroshima.* New York: Random House.

Loescher, Gil and John A. Scanlan
1986    *Calculated Kindness: Refugees and America's Half-Open Door,* 1945 to the
Present. New York: The Free Press.

Long, Lynellyn D.
1993    *Ban Vinai: The Refugee Camp.* New York: Columbia University Press.

Lyman, Stanford M. and William A. Douglass
1973    Ethnicity: Strategies of Collective and Individual Impression Management, *Social Research 40,* 344–65.

Malinowski, Bronislaw
1935    *Coral Gardens and Their Magic.* Bloomington: Indiana University Press.

Mitchell, Roger
1987    The Will to Believe and Anti-Refugee Rumors, *Midwestern Folklore 13*
(1):unpaged.

Mitchell, Roger, Touly Xiong, Charles Vue, Moua Xiong, and Leanne Martin
1989    The Eau Claire Hmong Community: A Cooperative Study, *Wisconsin
Sociologist 26* (1), 33–37.

Mortland, Carol A.
1987    Transforming Refugees in Refugee Camps, *Urban Anthropology 16* (3–4),
375–404.

Mottin, Jean
1980    *The History of the Hmong.* Bangkok, Thailand: Odeon Store.

Muecke, Marjorie A.
1987    Resettled Refugees' Reconstruction of Identity: Lao in Seattle, *Urban
Anthropology 16* (3–4):273–289. Special Issue: S.E. Asian Refugees in the
U.S.

Ngor, Haing
1987    *A Cambodian Odyssey.* New York: Warner Books.

Olney, Douglas P.
1983    *A Bibliography of the Hmong (Miao) of Southeast Asia and the Hmong Refugees in the United States.* Southeast Asian Studies Occasional Papers No.1, second edition. Minneapolis, MN: Southeast Asian Refugee Studies Project, Center for Urban and Regional Affairs, University of Minnesota.

Peterson, Sally
1988    Translating Experience and the Reading of a Story Cloth, *Journal of American Folklore 101* (399), 6–22.

Pfaff, Tim
1995    *Hmong in America: Journey from a Secret War.* Eau Claire, WI: Chippewa Valley Museum Press.

Portes, Alejandro and Rubén G. Rumbaut
1990    *Immigrant America: A Portrait.* Berkeley: University of California Press.

Portes, Alejandro and Min Zhou
1993    The New Second Generation: Segmented Assimilation and its Variants, *The Annals of the American Academy of Political and Social Sciences.* (November), 74–96.

Quincy, Keith
1988    *Hmong, History of a People.* Cheny, WA: Eastern Washington University Press.

Reder, Stephen, et.al
1983    *The Hmong Resettlement Study Site Report: Fresno, California.* Submitted by Northwest Regional Educational Laboratory, Portland, Oregon to the Office of Refugee Resettlement, Washington, DC.

Rumbaut, Rubén G.
1989    Portraits, Patterns, and Predictors of the Refugee Adaptation Process: Results and Reflections from the IHARP Panel Study in *Refugees as Immigrants: Cambodians, Laotians, and Vietnamese in America.* David W. Haines (ed.). (pp. 138–182.) New Jersey: Rowman and Littlefield.
1991    The Agony of Exile: A Study of the Migration and Adaptation of Indochinese Refugee Adults and Children, *Refugee Children: Theory, Research, and Services.* Frederick L. Ahearn, Jr. and Jean L. Athey (eds.). (pp. 53–91.) Baltimore and London: The John Hopkins University Press.

Savina, F. M
1930    *Histoire de Miao.* Hong Kong: Societe des Missions etrangeres de Paris.

Seller, Maxine S.
1987    Beyond the Stereotype: A New Look at the Immigrant Woman" in *From Different Shores: Perspectives on Race and Ethnicity in America.* Ronald Takaki (ed.). (pp. 197–203.) New York: Oxford University Press.

Smith, J. Christina
1988    *The Hmong: An Annotated Bibliography, 1983–1987.* Southeast Asian Refugee Studies Occasional Papers No.7. Minneapolis, MN: Southeast Asian Refugee Studies Project, Center for Urban and Regional Affairs, University of Minnesota.
1996    *The Hmong: 1987–1995, A Selected and Annotated Bibliography.* Refugee Studies Occasional Papers. Minneapolis, MN: Refugee Studies Center, Institute of International Studies, University of Minnesota.

Stein, Barry
1981    The Refugee Experience: Defining the Parameters of a Field of Study, *International Migration Review 15* (1), 320–330.

Strand, Paul J. and Woodrow Jones, Jr.
1985    *Indochinese Refugees in America: Problems of Adaptation and Assimilation.* Durham, NC: Duke Press Policy Studies, Duke University Press.

Stuart-Fox, Martin (ed.)
1982    *Contemporary Laos: Studies in the Politics and Society of the Lao People's Democratic Republic.* New York: St. Martin's Press.

Sweeney, Michael, et.al
1984    *The Hmong Resettlement Study Site Report: Portland, Oregon.* Submitted by Northwest Regional Educational Laboratory, Portland, Oregon to Office of Refugee Resettlement, Washington, DC.

Taft, Julia, David S. North, and David A. Ford
1979    *Refugee Resettlement in the U.S.: Time for a New Focus.* Washington, DC: New TransCentury Foundation.

Tapp, Nicholas
1982    The Relevance of Telephone Directories to a Lineage-Based Society: A Consideration of Some Messianic Myths about the Hmong, *Journal of the Siam Society 70,* 114–127.
1989    *Sovereignty and Rebellion: The White Hmong of Northern Thailand.* Singapore and New York: Oxford University Press.

Thao, Cheu
1982    "Hmong Migration and Leadership in Laos and in the United States" in *The Hmong in the West.* Bruce Downing and Douglas Olney (eds.). (pp. 99–121.) Minnesota: University of Minnesota.

Thao, T. Christopher
1986    Hmong Customs on Marriage, Divorce and the Rights of Married Women, in *The Hmong World I.* Brenda Johns and David Strecker (eds.). (pp. 74–98.) New Haven, CT: Yale Center for International and Area Studies.

Thao, Xoua
1984    Southeast Asian Refugees of Rhode Island: The Hmong Perception of Illness, *Rhode Island Medical Journal 67,* 323–330.

Tran, Thanh Van
1991    Sponsorship and Employment Status Among Indochinese Refugees in the U.S., *International Migration Review 25* (3), 536–550.

U.S. Department of Health and Human Services
1992    *Refugee Resettlement Program, Report to the Congress, January 31, 1992.* Washington DC: Office of Refugee Resettlement, U.S. Dept. of Health and Human Services.

Vang, Kao N.
1982    Hmong Marriage Customs: A Current Assessment in *The Hmong in the West.* Bruce T. Downing and Douglas P. Olney (eds.). (pp. 29–47.) Minneapolis: Center for Urban and Regional Affairs.

Vang, Tou-Fu
1979    The Hmong of Laos, in *An Introduction to Indochinese History, Culture, Language, and Life*. John K. Whitmore, ed. Ann Arbor: Center for South and Southeast Asian Studies.

Wain, Barry
1981    *The Refused: The Agony of the Indochina Refugees*. New York: Simon and Schuster.

Westermeyer, Joseph, John Neider and Tou Fu Vang
1984    Acculturation and Mental Health: A Study of Hmong Refugees at 1.5 and 3.5 Years Post Migration, *Social Science and Medicine 18* (1), 87–93.

Whitmore, John R. and Nathan S. Caplan
1985    *Southeast Asian Refugee Self-sufficiency Study: A Final Report*. Prepared for the Office of Refugee Resettlement, U.S. Dept. of Health and Human Services.

Winter, Roger
1993    The Year in Review, *World Refugee Survey*. (pp. 2–4.) Washington, D. C: U.S. Committee for Refugees.

Wyman, David S.
1968    *Paper Walls: America and the Refugee Crisis 1938–1941*. New York: Pantheon Books.
1984    *The Abandonment of the Jews: America and the Holocaust 1941–1945*. New York: Pantheon Books.

Xiong, May and Nancy D. Donnelly
1986    My Life in Laos in *The Hmong World I*. Brenda Johns and David Strecker (eds.). (pp. 201–243.) New Haven: Yale Southeast Asia Studies.

Yang, Peter K.
1996    The Hmong: 20 Years in Wausau, *Wausau Hmong-American News*. Volume 9.1 (April):7

Yang, See Koumarn
1980    The Hmong of Laos: 1896–1978 in *Glimpses of Hmong History and Culture*. Series #16. (pp. 3–17.) Washington D. C: National Indochinese Clearinghouse, Center for Applied Linguistics.

Zetter, Roger
1988    Refugees and Refugee Studies—A Label and an Agenda, *Journal of Refugee Studies 1* (1), 1–6.